I Don't Belong Here
A Year of Moving Forward and Essays on Grief
Becky Franzel

Aw Shucks! Publishing LLC

Disclaimer

This book is not intended to be a guide.

This book is not intended to give you any sort of definitive answer to all of your problems.

That is something you have to figure out on your own.

That said, I hope you are able to get something from this.

On August 13, 2016, I found my best friend and high school sweetheart dead of a self-inflicted gunshot wound. Suicide.

His name was Jake.

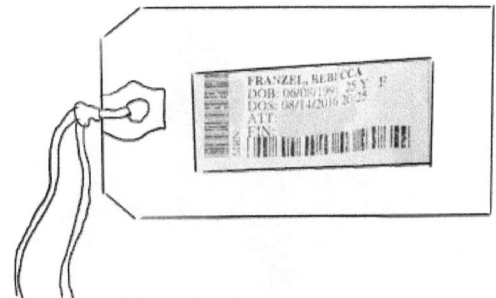

On August 14, I voluntarily admitted myself to inpatient treatment at a mental hospital.

On August 18, I was released in the morning. I attended Jake's funeral in the afternoon.

In Loving Memory of
Jake

Born to Life
May 25, 1991
Born to Eternal Life
August 13, 2016

*Jake's funeral card featured
a picture he had drawn of
Padre Pio, a Saint he idolized.
Padre Pio also struggled with
demons for most of his life.
While Jake was never religious
in the time I knew him,
his strict Catholic upbringing
carried into his adult life.*

After his funeral, I did not feel sad. I felt numb. While I cried at the funeral, it would be a lie to say that I fully understood what had happened. To me, it still didn't feel real. I felt like he was on a vacation, or that he was studying abroad, and would be back soon. As I did when he did travel, I started to write him letters. Instead of mailing or emailing them, I kept them. These are a few of those letters I wrote as I began to process it all.

***

August 18, 2016, after Jake's funeral

Hi, Dear,

Your funeral was not you. It did not seem like you, at least. I guess funerals never fully represent the person because they have to be thrown together last minute while the entire family is under total shock and stress. Especially when something like this happens. Everyone was pretty sad. They're not mad at you, though. I want you to know that. At least they don't seem to be.

I talked with Max, and he said he tried to get "The Imperial Death March" to play as your casket was taken away, but nobody would let him. Or maybe he was saying that to get a laugh out of me and didn't really ask anyone. Either way, I'm happy he did it.

I snus'd you—one pack of General mint snus, unopened. It's in your left pocket. Max left a dick pic in your casket, but I'm sure you've found it by now. You're not getting off that easy.

You're wearing your Red Fang shirt, your favorite one. Max and I are both wearing our Red Fang shirts. Mine is the cat one—the only shirt we have that's the same. I have yours now. I have all of your old band shirts, but I don't know what to do with them. I hope something will come to me soon. They still smell like you, even though your mom washed them. I have them in a bag right now, and I'm scared to open the bag. I thought you'd appreciate this. I always loved the way you smelled. Don't get a big head about it, though.

Anyway, I'm wearing black and navy blue together though, just to spite you (it does match, so fuck you, I look great). I tried to touch your hand but it was so cold and it felt fake, so I could only do it for a couple seconds. It was an open casket for only the very beginning, so not too many people saw you.

They did a pretty good job covering everything up, but man, it was SO not you. If anything, your cheekbones. I couldn't see your "perfectly chiseled cheekbones," as you used to say. I couldn't see your eyes and I couldn't see your cap-toothed smile, which to me made it look like the you I'd like to forget, the you that wasn't *you*.

It was also Bishop Hein's birthday, the bishop who traveled with you to Ireland when you were a kid (remember him?), so your mom made him a cake to celebrate. I don't think it has hit her yet, either, but I can't tell. I sat with Lindsay and Jessi and we ate cheese curds from Culver's and tried to keep each other laughing so we didn't start crying.

This all seems surreal to me, still. I'm still laughing and joking with you in my head, but it hasn't hit me that you're never going to respond yet. I hope you do, even if it's some creepy bodiless voice telling me I smell like poop when I'm trying to fall asleep. Even if it's fart noises when I'm taking myself way too seriously. Anything. I miss you so much, already, but I still feel like I'm going to see you again, that you're just in Germany or Thailand or wherever again and that you'll be back soon.

Love you forever and always, no matter what. Ladybug

P.S. I told your dad that you stole his dance move—you know the one. I know I said I'd never tell, but you're not here anymore, and I thought that would make him happy. I'm sorry, the cat's outta the bag now!

(Five days later, after lots of alcohol, I'm guessing)

Dear Jake,

Fuck you fuck you you fucking coward you said you wouldn't you promised me you wouldn't we promised each other we wouldn't lose it TWO WEEKS BEFORE YOU DID IT you said you had it under control and you lied you're such a fucking coward how could you do this to me? Fuck you fuck you fuck you fuck you you always said you were stronger than that but you were a weak spineless bastard fuck you fuck you fuck you

you just left me here how could you do that

(One day later, very hungover, probably)

Dear Jake,

I'm sorry, I didn't mean any of that. I miss you. I love you. Even if you're decaying by now, I want you to come back, like in *American Gods* where Dead Girlfriend comes back. I want Dead Boyfriend to come back. I still don't forgive you, but I'm trying real hard to accept it. I'm still mad at you, but I don't want to be. I want you to know I'm trying real hard to not be mad at you, and to see this as a mistake rather than something that defines you. It's really fucking hard though, okay?

I miss you and I love you, always and forever, dear. Even if I'm mad as hell at you, I still love you.

(Four weeks later, ish)

Hi,

I'm going to visit your grave today, but there's no headstone yet. I'm scared. If you could at least will some good weather for me, that would be great.

(Later that day)

Hey again,

I tried going to your grave but I couldn't get out of the car. I lost it. I saw where your plot was—furthest away, in its own corner, and at first this made me happy because I know how much you like your space but now I can't handle how alone you must feel. And I know you're dead but I don't know definitively that you don't somehow still feel loneliness, you know? Plus, the ground is getting cold. I hope you're not cold. I know this all sounds ridiculous, but I still can't accept it yet, okay? I can't accept that you're not still alive. That you don't still feel.

I hope you forgive me for saying I'd visit, but I just couldn't do it, okay? I'm not ready. That spot does not symbolize you to me. I don't think it ever will. I'll try to visit another time.

(I didn't visit.)

Dear,

Hey, did you know Nina Simone was bipolar, too? I didn't know that. Just thought I'd let you know. I remember you always used to say you hated her when I'd put her on, but man, some of her songs are really catchy!

I had another dream about you last night, and it was a good one. Not like the other ones I've been having. You're still not talking, but I hope you do soon. For whatever reason, it's just a bunch of consonants, but it's still good to hear your voice and to see your face regardless. It's not like we were doing much—just driving around the hills and woods in Merton, but we were happy. I woke up happy. If you did that, thanks for that. Miss you, love you, wish you were here.

(While I'm not certain, I'm guessing this was about a week later.)

Hey,

It's not getting easier. At all. I'm really trying, but I think I need some more time to process. I should probably cut off the alcohol, but I really don't know what else to do to turn off my mind. I don't want to take medication, but I guess alcohol is the same thing at this point. Is that why you drank so much, too? Is this how you felt then? I hope not. I really hope not.

I miss you, dear. I miss you so fucking much. I'm still so fucking mad at you for leaving me here, but I don't hate you for it. I hope you understand the difference.

I forgive you. I miss you. I love you.

(The following three were just a few written as I started drinking more [late October, early November]. Many were illegible—part from spilled wine, part from tears, part from being absolutely 100% out-of-body drunk while writing.)

Fuck you

Hi,

I meant that, you fucking coward.

Hey,

Sorry, I didn't mean that.

(In late November, I started writing him actual letters again. I cut back on drinking as I noticed it took over. As soon as I cut back—as soon as I had nothing to block out those thoughts—it became harder to write to him.)

Dear!

Concert tonight! Concert tonight! It's in Chicago, though, so that's a bummer. I'm going with someone, and I hope you don't hate me for that. I miss you, but I'm lonely. I have to move on sometime, you know?

Hi, Dear,

It was a good Chicago show, for once, but it made me miss you more, and now there's this guy sleeping next to me and I feel sick to my stomach so I'm curled up in a ball facing the wall and he's lying in the other direction so I'm pretty sure it's not gonna work out so you don't have to worry about that. I'm writing this under the covers, using my phone's flashlight, so I'm pretty sure he thinks I'm fucking insane. I'm okay with it.

Also, I'm pretty sure he's not interested after I started crying for no reason, or when I curled up into a ball and faced the wall and told him that I really wanted him to not touch me at all, not even touch feet, and that no, I didn't want to talk about it (I'm the worst).

I miss you and I'm sorry I didn't treat you right when you were here. The most painful thing for me is that I can never tell you how sorry I am and how much I forgive you. I really do forgive you. I do wholly and I just want you here with me and I want this to all be one bad dream and I want to go to George Webb with you and just talk it out over two cups of black burnt coffee like we used to.

Hi, Dear,

I'm okay, it's just it's really hard to keep talking to you like this. It's almost our anniversary, eight years in three days. I realize we didn't have the most consistent or stable relationship, but I still consider it eight years. Just thought you'd like to know. I miss you, but I'm really trying to get over you. I'm not sure if I'm ready, but I've gotta try because it's just getting to hard to sleep alone at night all the time.

I have dreams about finding you, you know that, right? Like, all the time. It fucks with me. I can't wake up alone to that anymore. Especially working from home, when I have no one there to get me out of my head. It fucks with me.

Merry Christmas, Dear,

Weird not doing midnight mass with your family. I miss them, but I think my family is happy to have me home. I remember that last year, you sat in the back with your Richard Dawkins book and I came back and sat next to you and you wouldn't talk to me, but you held my hand and squeezed it. I thought that meant you were okay, and maybe you were at the time. You can't answer me on that, now, so I guess I just have to assume you were okay then.

I stopped writing to him after Christmas, in a very strange, distorted New Year's resolution. It was my mission to heal. This meant moving on, which in my mind at the time, meant no more *letters*. I tried to start my life again after that, but I was fumbling. Almost every night I was dreaming about him, oscillating from finding him dead to memories to things we had never done before but planned on doing, then back to violent fights we had in the past, the dark times. In a strange way, I was able to distance myself after a few minutes, but they still lingered after I woke up and that's the part that stung.

I tried to date, but obviously, when you're having dreams like this almost every night, it never really worked out. I think if anything, I wanted that same connection again—someone to show me I wasn't as alone as I felt.

I'm not sure if I was scared to connect with other people or if I was scared of falling in love with someone else. They were all nice enough, and we got along well enough, but the disconnect happened whenever I started to feel too vulnerable. When I felt I would tell them too much, when I thought I would scare them away, when I realized they wouldn't live up to what Jake had been for me (which at this point I had completely romanticized and put on some sort of unreachable pedestal). It was obvious that I wasn't ready.

That, and the dreams. It's hard to wake up next to someone with the image of your dead boyfriend burned into your memory from only a moment before.

I tried to reconnect with people I had known before, but it always fell flat because I was too concerned with them worrying about me. I overplayed my happiness—a sad, pathetic, drunken clown. I became obsessed with convincing people I was okay, that I didn't need help, and that, like so many other problems I had faced in my past, I would be able to handle this on my own.

I couldn't.

Prelude

March 18, 2017—Madison, Wisconsin

I had no business being in that venue, a half-mile away from the house where I found Jake dead six months before. I knew that. I ignored that.

As I drove that once familiar path from Milwaukee to Madison, the manic "I have to do something" energy pulsed through my veins. When paired with nicotine and stale coffee, I could feel the muscles in my body twitch, electric, uncontrolled. Even though I knew going to this concert wouldn't change anything, I felt I had to do something for him. No, that I *needed* to. I convinced myself this was it.

Or at least, this would be a step in the right direction. A step further. At least a step away from my living room with a box of wine, alone, as I had done for the past six months. A step closer to closure, even if it was forced.

I had a plan. I would buy two tickets—one for me, and one for the memory of him. I would give his ticket away, in his memory. I would not say why or who it had been for. I would lie if asked. I would drink a gin and tonic, then continue the night with PBR tall boys, as he used to do. Because All Them Witches had been the last memorable band we saw in Milwaukee, one we had planned on seeing again, I felt this would finally, maybe, give me the closure I had been so desperately looking for.

And even as I planned this, I knew I was running in circles around his memory instead of progressing forward. I knew in the pit of my gut that this would get me nowhere. At this point, I didn't know what else to do or where else to go.

Moving in circles was better than getting stuck in place, I justified. *At least I was going somewhere.*

But no matter how many times I had played this moment in my head, I still wasn't ready.

The memories came back to me as soon as I entered the venue, but I tried to block them out. I thought of other things. I thought of the weather outside, gloomy. I actively focused on the people I passed, my immediate surroundings. I greeted my friend, Petrina, who was standing in the back, before going to the bar. I ordered a gin and tonic. I went to the front, by the stage, by the speakers, where it's acceptable to be alone simply because conversation is nearly impossible. I focused on nothing but the static coming from the speakers as the band set up.

And for a moment, I wondered where Jake was, until I realized he wasn't there. My gut clenched, calmed only by another sip of gin. This thought still sticks with me, no matter how much time has passed. The gut punch *Where's Jake?*

I tried to stop thinking about it, but at that point, it had infected my thoughts.

Focus on something else, I tried to tell myself. *Or focus on nothing*.

As they started to play, I closed my eyes and pretended I wasn't there, that I was at home. Safe. Holed up. I absently swayed to the beat blasting out of the speakers next to my ear, but other than that, I disconnected from the room completely. In my mind, I was floating above the crowd, watching.

I drifted to another concert Jake and I had seen here before—Movits!. I remembered we had gotten into an argument, only five feet away. I tried to black out the negative thoughts, but at that moment, I couldn't escape them. I tried to drink them away, but this only made his face clearer in my mind. This memory, his voice, warped into something I knew it wasn't. I tried to think of anything else, anything to distract me from this.

He isn't here to defend himself, I thought. *This isn't fair*, I thought.

Still, I could see his eyes in the back of my mind, piercing. I could hear his voice, cutting. To me, he was still here. This memory cut open a wound I thought had healed, then poured vinegar on it. All of the healing I thought I had done had disintegrated. In my mind, I regressed to the person I was the moment I found him, screaming nonsense from behind a chain-locked door at his dead body—helpless, alone. I tried to think of anything else, anything, but I felt as if I was falling down a set of stairs—each memory upon the last hitting me in the back of the head as I fell further down to where I was before.

Then, the singer sang something I understood. "Am I going down? Am I going up? Am I going nowhere?" And as all things said at just the right moment, this line shielded me from another stab of painful memories. A connection that acted as a shield, or at least a distraction. As I felt it, someone said it. There was a pause just long enough for me to push back my emotions and connect before he continued.

"I don't wanna wait too long, while I'm buried in the ground."

Even though I didn't know the rest of the words, I felt my thoughts drum to the beat of the music—completely in sync.

And at this point, I fully admit the alcohol was going to my brain. And at this point, I fully acknowledge I was looking for somewhere to run. At this point, I was a cornered animal escaping a ghost that had haunted me for the past six months—something that could and would kill me if I stayed here. If I stayed static.

When the mind is twisted, as mine was, it can convince you of anything.

I could not stay here. I could not stay in this city. I could not stay in this state. Unless I wanted to be haunted by this sorrow, I knew I had to leave.

The only thing I didn't know was where to go.

***

A week later. The wanderlust set in after a few glasses of boxed red wine, a stale Cabernet, filled liberally. Around me, I felt my apartment walls caving in, suffocating me. My ass indented into my pilled, gray, slouched couch.

Because I work remotely, I would be able to support myself while on the road without taking too many vacation days. My job is intense, but not so intense that I wouldn't be able to take it on the road. I researched wandering nomad groups—groups of people who work remotely and travel together—but I knew I had to do this alone, that I had to plan this alone.

"Well, I guess I could just see what cities that band is performing in, then choose from there," I thought.

It was something Jake and I had always talked about. His family was in music production, we were both into travel, and we were both into checking out new venues in new cities. I felt, if I were to honor him properly, this would be the way to do it.

After polishing off another glass of wine, I looked at what cities they would be touring. I saw New Orleans, and thought about how I had always wanted to visit that city. That if Jake had been here, he probably would have wanted to go, too, if only for the adventure.

I bought two tickets to see All Them Witches in New Orleans—one for me, and one for the memory of him.

Chapter One

On the road, listening to The Animals. My road trip go-to. And now, especially now, Eric Burdon's voice held all of the emotion I craved to connect with, even if I couldn't process the lyrics. I sang along to the melody, skipping half of the words as my mind deviated. I stopped singing and listened once my voice got tired, about an hour in. I switched to Black Sabbath and hummed along to about a fourth of what I usually would, mostly the instrumental parts.

The road was nearly empty as I drove south toward New Orleans. Though 50°, the sun made it feel almost 60°. The sun was at that point where it makes it nearly impossible to see anything, even with sunglasses, peeking at me from just under the sun visor.

The horizon turned redder as I drove toward it. The tree's shadows grew longer, like fingers stretching across the road.

My head was throbbing—partly because I hadn't been sleeping, and partly because I hadn't been eating much. For the past few months, my diet consisted of mostly cottage cheese, off-brand Triscuits, boxed wine, and a daily women's multivitamin as an afterthought (usually taken with a glass of that boxed wine at the end of the night).

While this was incredibly economical, and while this helped fund my trip, I felt like garbage. Compared to the old me, who carefully monitored her food intake on a near-neurotic level, health-and-sustainability-wise, I didn't feel like my normal self. Thinking logically wasn't an option simply because I didn't have the nutritional tools to do so. Partly because I didn't want to.

I was also 20 pounds lighter, weighing in at a staggering 110 lanky pounds. My clothes hung awkwardly. My cheekbones jutted. When people complimented me on my weight loss, I'd say tongue in cheek that I was on the "depression diet." It was weight loss through neglect—not through any positive, healthy changes I had made in my life.

I was going to see All Them Witches on a Friday, but I was staying with someone in Baton Rouge the first night, so I left on a Wednesday. I took off work, but told everyone else outside of work that I was going on a business trip. I told myself they wouldn't understand, but in my heart I knew what I was doing was ridiculous. I trust those around me. I knew they would tell me it was ridiculous.

But I didn't want to hear it.

This had become a routine for me. I wouldn't call it self-destructive, but I had grown accustomed to building a wall around what I felt was my recovery.

In my head, I was fine. I felt, like with everything I had done in the past, I would be able to take care of it myself, and only I could care for myself. I was healing, and like a hurt animal I retreated to my remedial safe space. For me, this safe space had always been the unknown—the open road, a city where I didn't know the streets and where nobody knew my name.

I was incredibly fortunate to have a reliable car—a 2016 Honda HR-V, with a back big enough to sleep and store my things in, if worst came to worst. I was not fortunate that this came from getting my old sedan stolen two months before Jake had died.

This turned out to be a positive. This new car did not remind me of the multiple times I drove to meet Jake in Madison or La Crosse or Merton, Wisconsin, or whatever other city he lived in at any point in the eight years I knew him, as the old one had. It did not remind me of the multiple times we drove to a show, no matter how treacherous the weather was. It did not remind me of all of the movies and George Webb dinner dates we did for, God, as long as I can remember, even when we were on one of our multiple "breaks." It did not remind me of the multiple subdivisions we'd park in, exploring the skeletons of houses under construction under a star-filled sky, making up stories about the people who would live there while also exploring our own futures, with Pink Floyd's "Animals" blasting from car speakers.

After you've known someone intimately for eight years, it's difficult to find a place that doesn't house a memory. Even the mundane details reappear in the most insignificant of places. Sometimes the most mundane are the ones that elicit the most violent responses—the ones you're most afraid to forget. The humanity of the person you've lost lies within these mundane details.

But this car was not connected to him.

My plan was to drive 15 hours straight. I would leave at 6:00 pm and drive straight through the night, to arrive right at sunrise. This was my goal.

Not that I minded—in fact, I preferred it. I had always liked night driving. I didn't need coffee. I had adrenaline, plus I had enough packs of nicotine in my lip to keep a horse up for a week straight. There were four packs of General mint snus, one shoved in each corner of my mouth. (In my head, it was nothing but pure. animalistic drive. It was a motive with unknown purpose.) That drive to do *something*, *anything* was there, but recovery almost seemed like a pipe dream. At this point, it was like a fix of temporary happiness, though I didn't realize it at the time. I don't think I would have cared if I had. I just wanted something to make me feel happy again. I wanted an escape from the sorrow.

As I drove past the Mars Cheese Castle, a gaudy monstrosity that is supposedly a notable Wisconsin tourist destination, I knew there was no turning back. That was my marker. I had never stepped foot in that place, but on every road trip I'd ever been on, I always used it as a mark—a point of no return. I rolled up my windows.

***

I always plan to listen to audiobooks on my drives, but whenever I get on the road, the last thing I want to hear is someone talking at me, no matter how engaging the story is. This trip, the *Lord of the Rings* trilogy would go unheard.

Even more now, I wanted something mindless. I wanted songs I was familiar with. I turned on Motörhead to keep myself awake, followed by Alice Cooper, followed by Etta James, followed by C.W. Stoneking, and Pokey LaFarge. To me, it was comforting to listen to other people sing about their problems. It was a distraction from my own, and was a point of relation for me. They made something of their pain.

At this point, for me, the entire subject seemed taboo—sacred. *Thou shalt not talk about it, as thou will not give an authentic, or genuine, enough representation*, I thought. Jake had been a living, breathing person, and to construct him into a cardboard cutout on paper seemed more insulting than ignoring his legacy.

Even though I wanted to, desperately, I felt I couldn't. I felt it was against some sort of rules I had set in my head. Undefined yet unbreakable.

I watched the trees come alive as I drove further south. Even though it was April, they were still skeletons in Wisconsin, recovering from a hard winter. As I drove south, everything slowly turned greener, fuller, livelier—at least vegetation-wise.

The further south I drove, I also saw more cars abandoned on the freeway. Not that this matters, but it is something I noted in my journal.

***

I finally made it to Baton Rouge around 9:00 am—far past sunrise. As soon as I entered the city, my phone lost reception, so I continued to drive around to find places where I could at least pull up a map.

I noted two drive-through churches, where you could give confessions from your car. I briefly thought about it, but instead I stopped in a gas station.

Even though I don't smoke, I bought a pack of cigarettes. I remembered Jake saying something about how you look crazy going for a walk or standing outside alone without a cigarette. I know this isn't what he meant—he wasn't telling me to pick up smoking. I knew on this trip I wanted to be alone, but not holed up in a room.

At least the smoke would drive people away from talking to me, I thought. I was okay with looking gross. After the past seven months, I was used to that.

Natural American Spirits—the yellow pack, like Jake used to buy. I lit one with snus still shoved in all corners of my mouth, gagged, then caught immediate head rush. My empty stomach protested, tired eyes shot open. I put it out immediately, but still kept the pack in my center console, where they remained for the rest of the trip, unused. At this point, that pack of cigarettes was all I had left to connect with him, so throwing them away felt wrong.

I would be staying with a friend of a friend and her husband. Their names were Jandee and Nate. Jandee was a pastry chef. Nate was a forensic investigator. They were both Mormon. (Not that it mattered. I'm not religious, but I'm also not anti-religious.) What did matter was that they had no idea what I had been through, so there was no chance it would ever be brought up. A fresh start.

I would be staying on Jandee and Nate's couch for a night or two, then I would figure out where I would stay in New

Orleans once I got there. I justified I'd want to see where was safe and walkable, but in all reality, I planned the trip so quickly that I didn't have time to work out those details. At the time, I don't think I cared enough—I was just looking for a place to run. But what I'd do when I got there, I wasn't sure.

When I arrived, I introduced myself and made brief small talk. Once they left for the day, I read for a bit, I wrote for a bit, then I crashed on her couch from noon until about 5:00 pm.

I woke up with two cats curled up on my torso, who stayed there as I stared at the ceiling, wondering what I was doing there. These thoughts were not panicked, but absent, as if I had no control over my actions or my situation. I recognized I was acting thoughtlessly, but I realized I didn't have control over my thoughts, so I felt helpless to where they led me. These thoughts lasted about 10 minutes, until Jandee came in the door and the cats jumped off to greet her.

We went to get po' boys at a local restaurant, and then the plan was to go back home and sleep. I was fine with that. Even though I just woke up from a nap, I was still exhausted.

The po' boy was good—shrimp. The conversation was good—dark. Nate talked about his work, so we talked about the macabre and grotesque, and the people and situations he encountered while on the job. How it changes from city to city. How New Orleans is different than Boston, for example, where he used to work. We also talked about the traffic, which was terrible. They told me it's because the city was built to be a small town, but when it exploded, they never updated the infrastructure. That infrastructure was always talked about during elections. Always the promise of improvement, but no promises fulfilled.

For me, this is exactly what I needed. Emotionless conversation—straight facts I could count on staying the same. Something I could engage with without giving too much information.

I couldn't tell if it was my brain overreacting to my *you don't belong here* thoughts I'd had since I woke up that afternoon, but I felt like the staff really didn't want us there. I hurried to eat my shrimp po' boy, and we left. We all fell asleep as soon as we got home. I slept dreamlessly. I woke up to one cat on my torso, again. It was 5:00 am.

I tried to fall back asleep, but I kept having those empty, falling dreams and the adrenaline would rush me awake. It was somewhere around 7:00 am when I woke up mentally, but somewhere around 8:00 am when I got up physically. I packed up my things and told them I didn't think I'd be back that night, and thanked them for the stay. I told them I would let them know if I changed my mind, but I didn't plan on it.

At this point in the trip, I only wanted to be a character in other people's stories. I didn't want them to get to know me too well. I only wanted to be a shell. I didn't know who I was at this point, so letting someone get to know me seemed like a waste of time. The human in me still wanted to connect. I recognized this, which is why my plan was to move as much as possible.

Thou must not grow roots, I thought.

Subconsciously, I was scared to process or admit what I was doing. I thought moving would keep people from getting to know me and getting to see what a wreck I was.

New Orleans turned out to be the perfect city to start this ideology. Everyone was eager to tell me their life stories, solicited or unsolicited. Nobody was interested in hearing mine, which I was fine with.

After I left Nate and Jandee's place in Baton Rouge, I went to the French Quarter. French Quarter Fest was just wrapping up, but its memory still lingered. In the trees, Mardi Gras beads were still hanging from bare branches, like Christmas trees decorated by a highly intoxicated mom after she had just gotten off third shift, half-assed. Musicians were everywhere. Some had instruments, and some made something up as they went along (using trash cans, sidewalks, and so on—all better than I could have dreamt of being).

"You can make more money busking than you can in any bar around here," the shopkeeper at a hat store I wandered into told me, as I was looking at the only pair of shoes they were selling—a pair of dramatic heels like I had seen in a music video at one point, but I couldn't remember the song or the artist.

"That's why most people busk. More money in it," he continued.

"You know, I used to be in a band. I play guitar. I play a *damn* good guitar, you know. Say, you like metal?" the shopkeeper said as I picked up one of the shoes. I set the shoe I was inspecting down and turned to him. Older—I'd say mid-60s. Short. Long, white hair. Top hat. Cane. Suit.

Even though he asked me a question, he stopped for a beat, then continued—his white beard stiff, just long enough to hit his bowtie jumping up and down as he spoke. "I used to be in [I've removed the band name]. Have you heard of them?"

I shook my head and was about to say something before he said, "We were real good, but then they got rid of me. Drinking problem. Trying to fix it, still. *Nasty* habit. My wife left me, too, because of the alcohol. *Nasty* stuff. You should stay away from it. Stay away from that green fairy!" He pointed a bony index finger at me, then laughed a hoarse croak.

For Jake, it had been the gin. I didn't want to say that, though. For me, too, I guess, at the end. I felt my eyes turning inward, analyzing my thoughts, so I forced them out by shutting off my mind. By focusing forward. Focusing outward.

That was when I noticed other customers trying to get into the very small, very cluttered store, but they couldn't move because we were in the way with our conversation that had just taken a dramatic turn downward.

"I'm sorry about that," I said, as I tried to back further into the corner, to let people into the shop and to steer away from the conversation. I didn't know what to say, and I thought he could tell, so I avoided eye contact.

Focus outward. Focus on the shoes. I noticed there was no platform for the toes to sit—just one straight-shot-down ballerina-style stilettos, with no platform for the toes to rest on. I noted how uncomfortable they would be as I thought of my own uncomfortable feet, sweating and swelling in boots meant for Wisconsin autumn.

"Oh, no need to be sorry." He held my shoulder for a second. "No need for sorry. They're shit without me anyway. I was only really with them for a few months, but they're shit without me now." He shook his head, laughed again, then, as if he had been talking about the weather, moved onto talking with the next customer.

I've gotta get out of here, I thought.

I walked back to the strip and wandered around the side streets until I found an Ethiopian restaurant to eat at. Out of all of the restaurants I could have picked, I chose the one where the idea is to be communal. I would be eating alone. I picked the smallest plate, something vegetarian.

As I ate, a painting hanging above the window stared at me, emotionless. I'm guessing it was done by someone who worked there, but I didn't get a chance to ask. I finished my food quickly, and though I had my notebook in front of me, I couldn't bring myself to write anything. It felt good to have food in me again. Real food. I left a tip and thanked them before leaving.

***

The All Them Witches show was outside of the French Quarter, in a residential area, where there were more coffee shops and bookstores than bars. As I drove into this part of the city, unlike the French Quarter, parking was free and plentiful.

I unpacked my toiletries from my bag and sprawled them on the front seat. I hadn't taken a shower, and I was just realizing how disgusting I felt and smelled. I sprayed my hair liberally with dry shampoo and tapped some powder on my face to hide the oil. I gave myself a very minimal shower with a face towel using water I had in my water bottle, rubbing the towel quick over my exposed skin, and prayed to every god I could think of that I wouldn't have a reason to lift my arms that night. I hoped my jacket would keep in the stench, though I could already tell it wasn't doing the trick. I rubbed the towel underneath my shirt in an attempt to get myself cleaner, but just as I started to do this, I saw someone staring straight at me, and it was unsettling. I stopped immediately and drove to a different spot before getting out.

My second parking choice was near a comic book shop I hadn't seen before. Whether I ever plan on buying something or not, I try to visit one in each city I visit. To me, no matter what city I was in, my mecca was always a comic book shop. Something I could get lost in.

Even more ideal, the shop was empty, the racks of books were tall and packed, and the shopkeeper wanted nothing to do with me. His nose was stuck in a copy of a comic I had heard so much about but had no

interest in—*Sex Criminals*. I'm sure it's great, just not my thing. And I certainly didn't want to get into another conversation about this comic that I'd never read, which seemed to happen a lot with *Sex Criminals* and me. I was happy he was quiet.

I went to the back of the store, toward the graphic novels. I've always liked those more than the superhero comics, the Marvels, or the DCs. I like my heroes fallible, clumsy, and whose arch nemeses were the demons they encounter in their everyday lives. Extra points if their demons actually defeat them. Relatable.

I guess I've never read Marvel or DC enough to know if this was accurate, but in my head, this felt right at the time.

I found one by a local artist who wrote something on the days leading to and the days following Hurricane Katrina. I had never considered those who had developed their personas around the city—those whose lives and livelihoods were not only *in* the city, but also *a part of* the city. *How many people had been through so many hurricanes and assumed this one would be no worse than the others they had survived.*

It followed three different story lines—one bar owner who was about to pass it to his son, one jazz musician nearing old age, and one woman who hadn't left her house in years. My mind delved into their own lives, their problems, their concerns, their hardships.

"Okay, I'm closing now, so if there's anything you want, I'm closing up in five minutes," the shopkeeper announced loud enough for me to hear without having to move from his seat.

I took note of the book's title and told myself I'd buy it later (then lost the scrap of paper), thanked him, and left.

The venue was just around the corner, covered in art with a fenced-in outdoor seating area, but the show would be in the bar indoors. I could hear them conducting a soundcheck, but it was still too early, so I decided to wander around a bit before the show. I had already bought my two tickets. I'd be fine.

I walked through a neighborhood nearby, pushing the *you don't belong here* thoughts to the back of my head. I thought of the book I had

just read. Then I noticed the water lines on the sides of the houses. I imagined what it would be like to stay here through that—the everyday life of watching it get worse and worse until you knew you had to leave, picking what you'd take, taking one last look at what you'd leave behind.

I wondered if anyone was happy to leave. I wondered if anyone felt positive about it. An excuse to escape, to start over.

I got to one house that reminded me of one I'd seen before—one Jake and I joked about buying when we were first dating, walking around Merton on a hot July day. It had been one of the few days we had off together over the weekend, and after spending the morning in the lake with our legs tangled in milfoil, we had nothing better to do than try to break into an abandoned house.

We weren't actually sure it was abandoned, but the rusted padlock and the thick fuzz of dust made for a fair assumption. Just inside the windows were boxes packed away but never opened. The grime-covered glass took a bit of elbow grease to clean just enough to see in. We cleaned meticulously while looking over our shoulders the whole time to make sure no one saw us, and we scared each other the moment one of us turned around. When I almost had the window cleaned, he scared me so bad that I cried—his two hands suddenly gripped to my sides and made me scream, and tears fell out impulsively. He never let me live that down, even years later.

We never got in. The turkey vultures, who nested in the nearby sanctuary, swarmed it in what we were convinced was an omen, so we kept walking. I remember my legs were stung from the nettle and whatever other weeds brushed up against them, but I didn't want to tell him because I didn't want that day to end. I wanted to keep walking. Even years later, we always stopped in front of it when we walked past it. *Our house.*

Narcissistically, I thought of a line I had written on that house a while back:

Gray, chipped smile of a sloping porch still stained by spit tobacco, Littered with sunflower shells and the memory of a rocking chair That creaked every time the wind picked up.

The most pain hides within the minutest details. The minutest details can be found anywhere, my conscience said over my poem, as I lingered in front of the house, absorbing the memory.

I walked to the Walgreens even though I didn't need anything and bought a pack of 5 gum, then walked toward the venue as the sun set. The sky, red.

***

At the concert, after I had given my Jake ticket away, I made sure to tell the bouncer to not say who gave away the ticket, and he gave me a weird side-glance. I moved past it.

I was about to get a gin and tonic at the bar, like I planned, like Jake used to, but I saw a version of an old-fashioned, which also reminded me of Jake. I changed my drink, assuring myself that this, obviously, would be the best way to honor his memory because we used to go to a bar in Madison that specialized in old-fashioneds. Sour, not sweet, like he used to get. *He was dynamic. My memorandums should also be dynamic*, I justified.

The drink was good, but it didn't make me feel as good as I had hoped. I switched to a gin and tonic as the opening band played. My head fogged as the alcohol hit me quicker than I thought.

I should have eaten something more substantial, I thought.

I saw the lead singer, Parks, and immediately panicked, and I came up with a reason I should be there. *You don't belong here*, my head shouted, but I blocked it out.

I had decided I was going to give the band a Milwaukee Comedy Fest notebook. This was partly because I was grateful for what they were doing, but also because I wanted them to feel appreciated, no matter how small the token was. I wanted to give them something special, something memorable. A token of my appreciation that they couldn't buy in a store.

Also, I felt if I gave them something it would give a reason for to me to be here. I didn't want to admit the real reason.

Parks said something along the lines of their band being sick in Madison and playing an awful show, and even though I don't remember most of the concert, I assured him they sounded great. He thanked me.

I walked back to the pit.

"I take a selfie with Parks every time I see a show. See?" A blonde-haired, wide-eyed kid said almost as soon as I got out of my conversation. "That's from 2014," he said as he turned his phone toward me. It was an awkward picture of him smiling and Parks looking like he had been ambushed. Blurry, as if it had been taken with a shaky hand.

I paused, gathered my thoughts, and said, "Ah, cool. I'm not really a picture person, really, but I'd bet the memories are—" but I don't think he heard anything I said. He continued his thought before I finished my sentence. My head was not there. My head was still in my purpose for being here. In Jake's memory.

"My friend says she made out with him, too. She's not here, though. I don't have a picture of that because I wasn't there."

"I don't know what to say that," I said as I took another liberal sip of gin—partly because I wasn't listening to him, but also partly because I didn't have the mental energy to connect with what he was saying.

I don't remember if the conversation ended there, but if not there, it was close to it. This is where I moved closer to the stage.

I talked with someone else about his home in Florida, about how he was in love with his girlfriend who couldn't make it to the show but he was sure he was going to propose to her soon. All said in one long, genuine, definite slur. I told him I was happy for him, but I'm not sure if he heard me.

As it had been when I was wandering New Orleans proper, I felt everyone simply wanted to tell me their stories rather than hear mine. Again, I was still fine with this—until I got into the bathroom and cried for five seconds, loudly, dramatically. Finally, an outlet. Like popping a zit that had been throbbing on my forehead all day.

"Everything alright in there?" A voice said to a newly open door. I stopped abruptly.

"Yeah, just stubbed my toe," I said, as if this completely justified my cries. I could tell she didn't believe a word, but she (very sweetly) said, "Okay honey, well, let me know if you need anything, or someone to talk to. Okay?"

I looked in the mirror. I hadn't been crying long enough to make my makeup run, but from here on out, I kept eyeliner in my purse. Although I knew I wouldn't see any of these people ever again, I still had my pride.

To counter my low, I went very high very quickly after taking a shot of whiskey. I made a bee-line to the bar, still wiping my eye. I bought one for the person next to me, and to assure him I wasn't hitting on him, I avoided all conversation and eye contact completely.

All Them Witches was playing, and again, to avoid conversation, I made my way to the front. This crowd was crazier, which made it easier to get closer (easier to flow with the crowd, to push forward with them).

I spent half of the show shouting the lyrics with a girl I didn't know and the other half helping a man I didn't know find his shoe, then helping him find his phone. I broke my boot heel, but not to the point of being unwearable.

Introspection hit me, then gut rot. I realized I hadn't thought of Jake during that show. I immediately felt guilty and wondered if I was doing the trip correctly. Because I had fun, I felt as if I had dishonored his memory, or as if I wasn't mourning right. I've had this feeling before, while I was in Milwaukee.

Something about traveling without him, experiencing new things without him, made me feel like I was overwriting memories we had together. I had been manic about recording our memories in the past seven months—I knew there was no one else to remember them with me anymore. The idea that I would be creating new memories without

him wasn't something I had thought about, and I didn't know how to process it.

Even though I only had one line addressing this thought, it haunted me for the rest of the time I was in New Orleans.

Where's Jake now? I thought.

Because I hadn't planned where I would be staying that night, I spent from 11:00 pm to midnight outside of the venue calling hotels. Because it was French Quarter Fest, everything was booked other than a hotel by the airport. I tried to haggle with the staff, and was able to get $20 off of an already overpriced hotel room. I drove there in silence, and once I got to my room, I laid in bed but did not sleep. I laid awake with no thoughts, staring blankly at the ceiling. My brain and body were tired, but they would not shut off. I got up to write, and what started as reflecting on my day deviated to a memory I had of Jake, one of the last positive memories I had with him.

July 2016. We had taken one trip to Michaels to buy supplies so we could make a REDRUM door ornament, red handprint and all, for all of the neighbors to see. This had been his idea. This was the last time I had seen him connected, engaged, excited—gathering a slew of inexpensive supplies to create the most authentic piece he could. In the background, we listened to Red Fang, who had just announced they'd be coming out with a new album in a few months. It was a tour we planned on going to. It was his favorite band, and my favorite band live. He never heard their new album. We never went to the show.

I had my own idea for a craft—something else I was going to make for the house, something to make it a home, but I don't think anything ever came of it. I bet if I searched through my boxes, still packed, I could still find the supplies, unused. Still in their original packaging.

I woke up in my hotel room at 6:00 am, then checked out at 7:00 am. I spent the next day wandering around the French Quarter market. I bought a harmonica from a man who called himself The Original Harmonica Slim, then a book some independent author was selling. I never read it.

I left around 3:00 pm I arrived home at 7:00 am the next morning. I slept soundly, with no dreams, for 10 hours.

Chapter Two

Two weeks after I had gotten back from New Orleans, I was now driving to St. Louis, Missouri, for another All Them Witches show. I left around 10:00 pm, four hours after I planned on leaving.

On the positive side, I was sleeping more. On the negative, that was all I was doing now. In Milwaukee, everything felt more real, especially coming back from the unknown. I was surrounded by things I knew, things we had bought together, and places we had gone together. Even my dreams were filled with memories, both the peaceful and traumatic. They ranged from some of our first dates to finding his dead body, replayed ceaselessly as I lay unconscious, paralyzed in a place I could not escape until I finally woke up.

After he died, I felt displaced, as if there was no reason for me to be here anymore. Though I knew I had loved ones here, I felt I had no purpose if Jake wasn't there.

Now, I would be traveling again, and I could not wait to leave. My plan was to drive through the night again, to arrive before I had to log into work that morning.

On this trip, I hadn't told anyone who truly knew me that I'd be going until I was already there. In my head, they didn't need to know. In fact,

I lied about it. I said I would be going somewhere else, doing something far more productive. I told my family I would be reading one of my short stories at an event for a local journal's publication, though it happened the week before. I skipped my cousin's baby shower because I was scared for them to see me this way—for them to see my dead, sunken eyes. I feigned moving forward, though I could feel myself regressing on hyper-speed.

I told everyone else, though—those I met at the bar, waiters, Lyft drivers, unsolicited. I wanted to tell someone, anyone, but I didn't want any backlash. I embraced the free-spirited costume, though my mind was chained to a memory. They didn't need to know that part. I left that part out. The moment they started asking questions was the moment I changed the subject to something else. Most of the time, it was the weather. Something that could be easily discarded and abandoned.

It was dark the entire drive, and the roads were empty. I was leaving on a Thursday, but this time, I didn't take off work the next day. I planned on working from the apartment I'd be staying in. I planned on keeping life going as usual. I couldn't address that I was running away from my problems. I thought I was fine, but the voice saying I wasn't was growing louder by the day, and my tears held more weight as reality started to settle in, though it hadn't yet, at least not fully. I tried to shut reality out by filling it with things to do. By traveling. By planning where I'd go next instead of focusing on where I was now.

I arrived at the Airbnb at 4:00 am, later than I had planned, and the host had told me the wrong room and left the wrong key. He left the key for his own apartment. When I entered with my overstuffed bag (10 books, two outfits, a few basic toiletries, one work laptop), I saw a man's shirt on the table, covered in crumbs from an open bag of off-brand potato chips, the bag sitting a few inches away. On the TV—motocross. In the bedroom—some sort of '80s synth-pop playing much too loud for this time of morning.

As soon as I opened the door, an alarm went off—one that made my eardrums rattle, my Jell-O legs, tired from lack of sleep and from sitting for so long, stiffened, prepared to run, though I knew I didn't have the energy reserves to do so. My brain, short circuiting from the seven-hour drive on no food, stopped and focused on the alarm.

The man living (or squatting?) there ran out of his room with only a pair of weathered cargo shorts on, bug-eyed. He was not surprised by me, but by the alarm. If I'm not mistaken, he said "hi" to me, as if this was a regular occurrence. He asked me if I remembered the code key, and I said I had no idea. He fumbled through a stack of sticky notes scattered on the table next to the lockbox and tried a few different combinations, until finally, the alarm stopped. He muttered something about putting the wrong keys in the lockbox, then grabbed the set of keys for the apartment below.

Because I was too tired to think about how precarious this situation was, I simply said, "Thanks." He asked if I needed help with my suitcase, but because my need to be alone was greater than my very desperate need for help, I said no. I spent the next 20 minutes maneuvering down the stairs. *Mind over body. Mind over body*. My arms cramped as I lifted my suitcase, and I regretted every single book I brought.

I picked this apartment because there were enough distractions here to keep my mind from wandering. From what I saw online, there were at least three Adonis busts, a white leather couch, a room full of mirrors, and a chandelier. When I got there, I also saw the full grand piano, the red velvet bed just below the chandelier that was bending the drop ceiling a bit too close for comfort, and after a bit of searching, a hidden office with two more busts (one Mozart, one I didn't recognize), two fox skins, and a fake velvet king's crown.

It was also the cheapest full apartment in St. Louis available that weekend, so that factored in as well. I was not only fine with it—I loved it. If anything, it made me feel a little saner.

After looking at the red velvet bed just below the chandelier, I decided I'd sleep as close to the edge of the bed as possible. Despite my surroundings, I fell asleep immediately and slept soundly, dreamlessly.

I woke up two hours later for work, before my alarm. I was not tired. I found a dusty tin of instant coffee, but to be honest, I don't think I needed it. It wasn't just pure adrenaline—it was that drive to do something, anything. I had found that thing in Madison, I tasted it again in New Orleans, and now I was searching for that fix again—that

feeling of "this will make everything better," if only for a moment. I was desperately grasping that last little bit of what I had of Jake's memory.

The concert was the next night, so I would have the day to myself to work and settle in. I spent my morning crying, turning off my tears to take calls, crying again, and drinking coffee. I took an impromptu half-day. Luckily, it was slow.

Around 2:00 pm, the man living in the room above me came down to see if everything was alright, still not wearing a shirt, still bug-eyed. I wouldn't be surprised if he didn't get any sleep. I would be surprised if he ever got sleep, actually.

Though he had all of the elements of being someone I should not trust, the way he spoke and the way he stayed on his side of the door entrance, without entering the apartment, kept me from ending the conversation abruptly. When he made eye contact, I saw he had kind eyes, despite his first impression, despite the bugginess.

At this point, it was also nice to have someone to talk with, though I wasn't sure he was hearing anything I was saying. It was nice to have a distraction from my thoughts. They were ebbing and flowing from Jake to my own basic bodily functions, which I had been neglecting. This ebb and flow—it was a strange animalistic urge, oscillating from mental to physical to mental again, though my methods for coping with both contrasted. It's difficult to feed your brain toward recovery when there's nothing feeding it. It's difficult to feed it when your brain is actively making you feel sick to your stomach.

Talking with this man, who I'm not sure even told me his name, was a welcome distraction from my thoughts. I'm not sure if he recognized this or not.

I asked him for restaurant recommendations. I had nothing but some stale mixed nuts and dried fruit I found in the pantry, washed down by way too much instant coffee and nicotine. I'm sure I looked just as bug-eyed as him—we were strung-out comrades, worn down, driven by something inhuman.

The only recommendation that stood out to me—he mumbled most of his responses—was one that was on Broadway, which he sung with the

tenor of an aspiring opera singer. I'm not sure if he even said the name of the restaurant, but he put all of his energy into singing the street name—a parody of a wayward drama student, with one arm raised in mock grandeur, his slacked stomach flexed as he rose his arm.

I pretended to listen to him intently, but I couldn't follow anything he was saying. I was still stuck on him singing Broadway, and I was still half-jokingly unsure if I was supposed to respond in song. I decided against it and said "thanks." He mumbled something, then shut the door, a look of sudden confusion on his face.

The difference between St. Louis and New Orleans, in my mind, was that people just wanted to talk, whether there was a story or not.

Again, I was fine with that. I could relate to that. I went to the living room.

The only thing I had kept constant since Jake's death was my daily Pilates practice—the only thing keeping my mind somewhat centered. My gut cramped as I held the boat pose—my muscles had nothing feeding them, nothing substantial at least. I moved to roll-ups, spine twists, then pushups. My body protested, but in true form, it was muted. I drove through it. *Mind over body*, I thought.

My eyes sagged, so I drank more coffee instead of taking a nap. My thoughts were unsubstantial, but they were spinning, like a flock of monarchs who had lost their coordinates. I ate more mixed nuts I found in the pantry and wrote for a few hours, but nothing substantial. I fell asleep shortly after, my body defeated. Shattered.

***

I woke up the next day and drank instant coffee again. Had mixed nuts again. Found something in the freezer—something reminiscent of ice cream, but I quickly found out it was nothing of the sort. I spit it out. I did Pilates. When I decided to take a shower, I found the shower head detached from the wall, hanging in the claw-foot bathtub, so I held it over my head and rubbed shampoo all over (I forgot soap). As I contorted to shave my legs, I was happy I had done some sort of Pilates, anything to warm my body up to keep my balance so I wouldn't

knock over one of the statues and busts stationed on every corner of the tub's thin, porcelain edge. I tried to sing to get my spirits up but only a croak came out—a bluesy, exhausted, single note. Monotone.

I went through the motions as I went over my plan for the night. I knew I would be drinking, so I didn't want to drive, especially in a city I didn't know. I was trying to save money, too, so I decided I would walk. I at least had that sense in me. Some reason.

Until it started pouring rain at 4:00 pm. It was pounding rain, hitting the glass windows so hard I had to check to make sure it wasn't hail. I called a Lyft to the venue, and planned on walking somewhere nearby for food.

But my plan of asking the Lyft driver for restaurant recommendations was immediately foiled when the driver decided to tell me all about how Walmart steaks are just as good as any other.

"You just throw it in the oven and you bake it. That's all you have to do," he told me. "I have one every day."

I decided maybe I'd just find a place to eat on my own. Google it, or something. There had to be something.

Around the venue, there was nothing but the rain, still pouring. The building was isolated, surrounded by offices and vacant buildings.

"Here you go," he said, as he let me out at an empty parking lot, with no sign showing the venue. "Have a good day," he said, before I could ask if he was sure this was the place. I saw a van unloading equipment, so I walked toward that. Luckily, I was right, but the venue wasn't open for another three hours.

The people unloading the van recommended a ribs place down the road, Pappy's, so I decided to go with that. Easy, at least, I thought, and I *had* to have St. Louis ribs, or so they said. I tried to order another Lyft, but I saw the same driver pop up in my queue, so I decided to walk.

I looked up the directions on my phone and walked a mile in the rain, down a busy street with no other pedestrians in sight. Cars passed me, each in their own world, wipers on high swipe.

I ordered ribs and pulled pork, and it was just as good as they promised me. I would have welcomed any food, but it was nice to have good food. Something substantial.

I stood at a table alone. Someone asked if he could take my chair for their table, and I was at a high-top, so I didn't really care. The waiter came by to pour new water every time I took a sip, even though there was a line of customers out the door.

"Thanks," I said as he poured my water for the fifth time. Another set of tired, kind eyes, then he nodded. *Comrades*, I thought again.

It's difficult for me to make assumptions about these different cities in retrospect because I know my mind was changing so much at this point, and so was my approach to others. I'm sure people are the same everywhere you go. I'm sure, at this point, I was so desperate for a connection that I noticed such connections more readily.

But to me? New Orleans is the city of unsolicited stories, and St. Louis is the city of tired, kind eyes, and there's nothing you can say that will convince me otherwise.

***

Outside, it was still raining. I decided to go downtown in search of my mecca—another comic book shop. This one was much larger, better lit, with two smiling cashiers at the front caught up in a conversation about a new comic that had just come out. I went to the back and looked at the graphic novels, as I always do, and stood back there for an hour re-reading one I already owned—Guy Delisle's *Jerusalem*. I reached one of my favorite parts, where Guy was trying to put his baby to sleep amidst prayer sirens in Jerusalem, when a woman in the shop asked, "Do you need help with anything?"

I should leave, I thought, but I focused on focusing my eyes and my thoughts outward. *You're getting too into your head again*, my thoughts countered. I concentrated on engaging—on connecting with the world outside of my head.

We made small talk about Guy Delisle, about how neither of us are sure of how to pronounce his last name, but we have read everything

he's ever written. We agreed that his style didn't immediately draw us in, but it fit the more you read it. I said, "Thank you," and left.

More coffee, I thought. I walked next door and bought more coffee. There was a miscommunication and the cashier gave me a large, but charged me for a small. I said I'd pay for the large, but he protested. I sat at a chess table—the only place with a chair. I listened to the cashier and a person who I assume was his boss talk about the pricing, and I couldn't tell if the owner was trying to train him or trying to fire him without making me feel uncomfortable. This went on for 20 minutes, and as I sat in silence, I wished I had brought a book. I let my mind deviate for a minute, to the time Jake had given me a graphic novel one Christmas with the disclaimer, "This is the best one I could find. I'm borrowing it when you're done," then reigned it back in.

I focused on my plan for the night.

I had already bought both of our tickets—one for me, and one for Jake's memory. I did this right after the New Orleans show. I already knew I would give one away, with the note, "Do not under any circumstances tell anyone who gave this ticket away" to the bouncer. At this point, this was routine. I anticipated the uncomfortable, wary side-glance from the bouncer, but I was used to that, too.

"Are you sure you don't want to give it to one of your friends?" he might ask, and no matter how much my tongue wanted to say, "I don't have any friends here. It's for the memory of my dead boyfriend," I would simply say, "No, give it to someone else, thank you."

I was so focused on not giving anyone information that it had never crossed my mind that maybe they wouldn't even ask—that maybe they didn't want to know, or maybe they would brush it over. Because it was in the center of my mind, I assumed it would be in the center of everyone else's if I told them. I decided to hold this within me, like some sort of distorted Christ figure. I would shoulder my own burden—it was no one else's but mine. I had to save them from my own pain and my own sorrow.

This time, I planned my distraction for the band, to keep them from asking why I was there again. I couldn't just give them another

Milwaukee Comedy Fest notebook—this time, I crafted a letter to my friend Petrina's sick dog. She said she would be joining me in St. Louis, but then couldn't because her dog was sick. I took that idea and ran with it. To me, this was the perfect justification of "Why the fuck am I here?", though, in retrospect, it made no sense.

I reviewed it.

I hope this makes sense, I thought. *I hope they don't ask too many questions*, I thought. My plan was still to not grow any roots, but it gets tricky when you're following the same people from city to city.

I finished my coffee, then ordered a Lyft to the show (still raining, harder than before). The drive was silent. I kept to myself, arms folded across my chest, looking out the window, making mental bets for which raindrop would fall the fastest down the window.

***

I entered the venue—one large room, reminiscent of a middle school dance floor. Low lighting. People stood in small clusters, though some sat at the benches on the back wall, in their own worlds behind their phones.

They were faces I didn't know, but I expected that. I told the bouncer to give my second ticket away, but he didn't even blink before saying, "Sure, cool. Next person without a ticket gets it. Thanks."

Though I didn't want to talk about it, I was taken aback by how comfortable the bouncer was with my request, compared to my previous experiences. I stopped for a moment, collected my thoughts, then I kept walking.

I thought about talking with people, then decided against it. They didn't seem interested, and to be honest, the sudden influx of food was making me tired, and I would rather take a nap on the bench than talk about what I thought the openers would be like with some stranger. I didn't know either of the openers, so it would be speculation.

Instead, I ordered a gin and tonic at the small bar the venue had, and it came in a plastic cup, much smaller than I anticipated.

I thought of how Jake always complained about venues with small, overpriced drinks, but I pushed this thought back. Instead, I turned to the bartender and said, "I'm going to need a lot more than this for what I paid," half in jest. He laughed, and said something along the lines of, "That was quick," after I took a big sip. I smirked, half-serious, and moved to the side of the bar so I wouldn't be blocking anyone else.

I finished this drink, standing by the bar, alone, then ordered another one promptly after. It had been about 20 minutes, and the bartender gave me a side-glance before giving me another one. I could feel my tongue wanting to say, "This one is for my dead boyfriend, Jake," but I didn't, thank God. *If anything, Jake would have hated the attention*, I thought.

I promised him this would be the last one, but I'm certain he didn't give a shit. Or, if anything, he was disappointed I wouldn't be buying more. *He doesn't give two shits about me*, I thought. Not angrily, but as a self-confirmation, to level myself.

I didn't know what to do with my hands, so I pulled out my phone, though there was nothing on my screen to look at. Messages—empty. Email—full of spam. I flipped through it for a moment, then put it back in my purse.

Though I fully understood I was traveling alone, I didn't realize how alone I'd truly feel. At least when I traveled alone before, I could always text Jake, and I knew he'd answer.

Now, I didn't even have that.

Traveling alone like this had made me incredibly egocentric in the most self-loathing way—I assumed everyone was watching me, judging me, as if they could read my thoughts as subtitles as I went through every action. That they could detect each mind deviation. I had begun focusing on focusing my eyes outward. Focused on making connections outside of my head, even if I didn't engage.

***

I saw the keyboardist, Allan, at the merch stand, so I walked up with my crafted card in hand. My purpose for being here.

But when I got up there, it didn't feel right. I held the card in my hand as we talked about the opener, Ranch Ghost, from their show in New Orleans. He asked me what I was doing, why I was here again, and I gave him vague details. I said I was traveling from city to city. He told me he lived in an RV for a while, and asked if I was doing that. I said no.

He didn't ask a ton of questions, and it's possible he never would have, but as soon as more questions started to appear, I brought out the card as a distraction.

As soon as I brought the card out, I felt my personality shift—it was a persona. I tried to level it out by saying, "I know it's stupid," but because this was my self-protection method, I felt myself falling behind a different skin. A more sociable skin. For as long as I could remember, I've always done that with humor, but I could always control it in the end—and at this point, I felt my personality shifting with it, uncontrolled. I was conscious of it, but I felt helpless trying to defeat it. It was more powerful than me. My natural persona was weak, hidden in the shadows of this carefully crafted version of myself that I made in my head.

I have always been fascinated with celebrities who get stuck in their stage persona—Alice Cooper, Ziggy Stardust, and the like. I never

thought I would become one; or, rather, a pathetic version of that. While I had never understood it before, I felt like I could relate to them now. It was comfortable. I understood it. It's easier than dealing with my reality—to inhabit a superhuman persona rather than exposing my weakened self to strangers. It was a better version of myself, I justified, even if it was crafted and disingenuous. It was something to hide behind when the going got too tough. Even better, this persona was portable. Invisible. I could take it anywhere.

"What is this?" Allan said, looking at the card I handed him.

"My friend was supposed to be here, but her dog got sick, so she couldn't make it. I made a card for her. I was wondering if you would all sign it," I said, my eyes focused on the card, analyzing every weird thing I had written in there.

Something dumb about Petrina's sick dog, Bruno.

Some see this glass as half empty

Some see this glass as half full

Equally dumb original message scratched out.

"It would mean a lot to her," I lied. I knew she would hate me for doing this. She was going to be incredibly embarrassed. (She was—sorry, Petrina.)

Surprisingly, they were into it (or at least pretended to be), and they all signed it. *Maybe they're just as tired as I am*, I thought. *Maybe they don't want to think about it too much, either*, I thought. I imagined they could

read my thoughts again, so I directed my attention to the merch guy. I made sure he signed it, too.

Parks brought up that Allan had taken the notebook I gave him in New Orleans. Allan brought it out of his coat pocket, and I felt my eyes retreat into my head, analyzing my *thou must not grow roots* mantra. I felt a connection to a past self, a self I wanted to push under the rug, though it was only a few weeks ago.

I forced my eyes to focus outward again and said, "Oh, that's really awesome!" I brought out my own notebook from my purse to change the subject, a faux-leather one, and when he said it was too fancy for him, I immediately became defensive, more defensive than I should have.

Like a cornered animal escaping her demons.

But I tried to blow it over. "I like it because the pages are bigger," I said. We talked for a bit longer, then I wished them good luck and made my way near the front of the stage again, by the speakers.

The only place where it's socially acceptable to be alone simply because conversation is nearly impossible.

Except this time, I noticed those around me—everyone knew someone. Everyone knew each other. I shoved my hands in my coat pockets and stood waiting for the opener. Unlike before, unlike New Orleans, I felt lonely—an aching loneliness. I was aware of my loneliness, and it festered in the back of my mind. I tried to block it out, but alcohol made that line blurry, and it crept into each thought I had.

I don't remember who the first opener was, but I remember not liking him as a person. Fake, I thought, but I guess I wasn't too much better at this point.

I spoke with Jake in my head: *This is the kind of guy you used to yell at.* But then I checked myself—

This is someone you would have yelled at when you were losing your mind. In your right mind, you would have never yelled at him because, in your

right mind, you were better than that. You were not that person. In your right mind, you wouldn't have wanted to hurt anyone.

I tried to be a better person, to listen and engage with the music. I couldn't, so I grabbed another drink. This time, a beer. I tried to focus on anything but Jake. *Focus outward. Look forward.* The floor wasn't that full, so it was easy to grab a drink and return to my post by the amps again.

The second band was playing, and I remember liking them as people, but I don't remember much of their music. Poppy. Fun. But I was too distracted to connect. It was background music to my thoughts, shouting in my head at 100 decibels.

I drank my beer—the cheapest one they had. I sipped it as I noticed the floor become more crowded as more people showed up. A lot of people were talking loudly, or were staring at their phones, faces illuminated by screens.

Man, that must suck pouring your heart out on stage, then looking out into the crowd to see no one giving a shit, I thought. I had experienced this with writing, but with writing, you usually don't have a direct connection with your audience. Usually, you submit a story, and it gets rejected or ignored. You don't see the rejection immediately—it's distanced.

Though I didn't connect with their music, I made a conscious effort to pay attention, to focus. At this point, I wasn't thinking about Jake—I was concerned about my surroundings, those around me. *Focus outward*, I thought, as I consciously connected my eyes to something outside of my head. I wanted to be sure everyone was fine, mainly the people on stage. I applauded louder than I should have when they said goodnight. I felt self-conscious of this, as if they heard me and assumed I was being demeaning. How I was acting was demeaning, but I didn't care. I wanted to make sure they were happy, that they felt loved. That they were comfortable.

A projection. I didn't feel comfortable, so I went to great lengths to try to make everyone else more comfortable than I felt. Often times, because I was incredibly uncomfortable, this came off as incredibly manic.

"Wow, that was great!" a man next to me said as soon as I was done applauding, and I didn't say anything back. Not because I didn't want to, but because I didn't know what to say. I sent him a "cheers," but didn't continue the conversation. He deviated back to his friend group, and I wondered if I had offended him. I hoped not.

All Them Witches came on stage. The songs they played became my comfort—while slightly different every time,

I knew them. I knew I would like them. I knew they would put on a good show. I got lost in it, and lost in everyone else's excitement.

"This is the first time I'm seeing them! Oh my God! Great!" one woman told me, older. "Have you seen them before?"

"Yeah, a few times," I shouted over the music. "Always a good time!" I made eye contact with her. Another set of tired, kind eyes. A connection. She started singing along to one of their newer songs, and I joined her until she went to go find her boyfriend or husband or lover or whatever. I was able to switch to my fun persona much more quickly now—in a matter of seconds, as the songs I knew played, it was much easier. Once she left, I took it off.

I was alone again, but now, I had the songs to connect with. I sang along on my own, probably a bit too loudly, a bit too passionately. It felt good to release something. Anything.

Another thing about traveling alone, or when you isolate yourself—you don't talk a lot. It feels good to use your vocal chords once in a while. This is completely separate from feeling lonely—it's like stretching a muscle you've neglected. I closed my eyes and sang along, and got lost behind the music. Another connection.

Once they had finished their encore, I called a Lyft immediately, but the estimated time was 14 minutes. I waited outside and, as the rain still poured, I watched the arrival time jump up 10 minutes. I was waiting in a small doorway away from the entrance, the only other place with a roof, where another guy was waiting for his ride.

"What a great show, huh? Have you seen them before?"

"Yeah, I've seen them a few times," and where I would have normally stopped, I continued. "I just saw them in Madison and New Orleans, too. Always a great show. Such good musicians."

"Oh shit, where are you from?"

"Milwaukee," I said. "I drove here two nights ago."

"Shit, why?" he asked, looking at his phone, one brow raised.

Again I wanted to say, "Because it was the last band my boyfriend and I saw before he died, and I really feel like I need to do something for him. This feels right, like the right thing to do."

Instead, I said, "A great way to see the country."

He didn't respond. His ride was on its way, and he walked away.

He thinks I'm crazy, I thought, but I pushed this to the back of my mind, where I housed the rest of my negative memories, and moved past it.

This time, I talked with my Lyft driver. We talked about music, about how lyrics just weren't as good as they used to be. How everyone got so wrapped up in superficial emotions rather than fixing their own problems.

"That's why I like this band. They talk about problems that don't go away. I have problems that won't go away, real problems that fester," I told him. And normally, my Midwestern roots would have told me this was giving away too much information, but at this point I felt I needed to say something.

And instead of imploring, he said, "That's deep. Heavy. I get that, man. I get that." He made eye contact with me via the rearview mirror. "Those problems will get better though, with time. You just gotta wait it out. You just gotta wait it out. It'll get better."

This is all I wanted to hear. It *will get better*. Even though I'm not sure if I believed him. At this point, as everything became more real, as the loneliness began to set in, I was falling deeper, and I recognized

that as best as I could with the state my mind was in. In my drunken state, I wanted to ask him when, but I didn't want to turn this into a therapy session. Once he got to my place, I thanked him and wished him goodnight.

I couldn't fall asleep that night, so I watched the Weather Channel. I focused on what the weatherman was saying, about the storm, but I didn't process it. I pushed it to the back of my mind, back with everything else. The raindrops pounded on the window, like someone banging on a padded door, muted.

I had read something about when you're in a new environment, it always takes you longer to sleep, naturally, because your body is picking up every new sound and gauging whether it is a threat.

I heard the man above me walking. I counted his steps. I heard the wind outside, rattling the window panes. I heard the rain pound against the wall and I wondered if I should even be here in the first place. I wondered when I would feel comfortable at home again, or if I would ever find a place that truly felt like home and just settle down. I was tired, but I was restless.

At some point I fell asleep, and I only know that because I woke up to birds chirping outside my window at 9:00 am.

Because I was here, I decided I had to do all of the things I told people I should do. To do all of the tourist stuff people had recommended—if anything, to justify why I was here to them, too. I walked downtown to get the special St. Louis pizza, but found the only place in town that didn't serve *provell* on their pizza (a combination of provolone, cheddar, and Swiss cheese that is particularly popular in St. Louis). I went to a blues night, but the band was preoccupied with telling everyone how their bassist had ditched at the last minute, so that's why they didn't sound good. I thought they sounded fine until they started justifying. I told the bartender this, and he shrugged without saying anything.

I left the next morning. I got home around midnight on Sunday. I worked at 8:00 am on Monday morning.

Chapter Three

It had been a month since St. Louis, and I had spent most of this time going backwards. More alcohol, less socializing. More lying in bed, less sleeping. I rarely left my apartment, but when I did, I felt myself fall into the persona I had crafted before. Unlike in St. Louis, I now found it more difficult to take off, like peeling a Band-Aid off an open wound.

It felt worse and worse to return to my weak self, without the mask, so I kept it on as long as I could. *A pathetic parody of myself,* I thought. I did not tend to my wounds. They festered behind this crafted character, and grew worse. When someone started to notice, I simply ignored their calls and told them I was too busy. My mask grew stronger as my true self grew weaker, more desperate for help.

And I knew I needed help at this point, but I couldn't bring myself to get it. I didn't know where to start, or where to go, without making anyone more worried for me than they already were. I didn't want to hurt anyone else. I thought that admitting a need for professional help would be to tell those around me that they weren't enough, that I didn't appreciate them enough, that they had failed me. I felt that talking about my problems would worry them more. I knew that I wasn't fine.

I wasn't close to being fine.

But I wanted to convince them I was.

I knew those closest to me could tell, but I pretended not to notice. I brushed off their remarks as crazy, then changed the subject. I didn't realize at the time that this sense of denial was likely hurting them more—making them more worried for me. Because I was so focused on the surface, I didn't see this. Because I wasn't wholly connecting, I didn't pick up on this.

Now, most of my flashbacks were of finding Jake, or of one of our fights near the end, when neither of us were in our right minds. Manic. Confused. Panicked. While it had started in my dreams, those dreams now lingered for most of the day. I was still working from home, so I was in my own head all day. Even when work was busy, it was difficult to pry those images out of my head when I never left my apartment.

They say the mind changes when you change scenery. You remember different things when you change environments. My apartment was becoming a constant reminder of what had happened, of the past. I was scared to escape it. Even more, I felt like I *could not* escape it. I didn't want anyone to see I was hurt. Once the mask was off, I didn't want to escape from my hole.

I still had some of his stuff in my apartment—a bag of his old band shirts, a large plastic bin that I still haven't opened, things from his apartment that his family thought might be mine. I'm still not sure if any of it is mine. I kept it in a closet in my office, far from sight but still close in my mind. Before, I had been able to ignore it. Now, like Poe's "The Tell-Tale Heart," I could sense it, even if I couldn't see it.

And now, everything reminded me of him. I was living across the street from a George Webb, which had been our favorite dive diner. I listened to the same bands we listened to, even the ones I didn't like. I revisited stories I had written—ones he had said he liked, even if I wasn't attached to them. And I reread old journals from our many trips together, like the one where we traveled from Germany to Belgium to Ireland. I honed in on any sign that he had been thinking of this before, any Easter eggs he may have dropped that he was planning on killing himself.

I reviewed what I could remember of our last conversations. I became obsessed that this had been my fault, and only mine. That I had missed something.

We had gotten into a huge fight, mostly my fault, and we decided it wasn't healthy to see each other—not even friends—less than two weeks before he killed himself. While I had assumed before, I was now convinced this was his way of distancing himself, that he had already decided at that moment—the moment he told me to get out. I reread the emails we had exchanged, and the text messages, and listened to the voicemails. Even the painful ones. Even the manic ones. The ones that cut me the most.

Every word I remembered him saying turned into some sort of distorted clue. Every memory turned black—even the ones I cherished the most, and even the early ones. I assumed he was trying to tell me he would do this. That I had missed something.

While I had thought about it before, I became obsessed with it now.

***

Cleveland. June 2017. This time, I told everyone I would be going, mostly because I would be staying with my brother, Jimmy, and my sister-in-law, Katie. This was planned. I knew I had to stay somewhere I knew, with people I knew.

I was not scared I would do something to myself. Even at my lowest point, I never seriously thought about killing myself. At my lowest state of mind, when those thoughts crept in, I knew I would never actually do it. It was more the fear of losing my mind. I wanted to be around those who knew me and wouldn't judge me. It would still be an escape, but at least it was an escape to a place I knew, with people I knew, compared to previous trips.

I had just had my birthday, and Jimmy's birthday was coming up. We decided we would celebrate, and then I said I would take them to a show. All Them Witches, again. This time, I did not give my extra ticket to a stranger, but to Jimmy. I didn't tell him this part—that I had been giving away a ticket to Jake's memory for every show I had been to. I didn't even tell him that I had already seen this band.

Before the show, Jimmy, Katie, and I went out for drinks and appetizers. I drank one Long Island Iced Tea and one Moscow mule, which would have been fine had I eaten a little more and not smoked. Also, as someone who usually sticks to two-ingredient drinks (gin and tonic, whiskey-ginger), I had no idea what a Long Island truly entailed. That's separate from losing my mind. That's just inexperience.

My head was hazy from the heat and alcohol. We caught up. They talked about what they were doing in Cleveland. They talked about the restaurant we were eating at, a new outdoor Mexican restaurant that shared a patio with a neighborhood pub. I told them about a short story I had just published, how I panicked when I read it in front of others—a college theater full of people. How I stuttered through the whole thing. How I was so nervous, I almost cried. We laughed, and it felt good. I hadn't laughed in a while. No matter how much I wanted to say that, I didn't, but I'm sure it showed in my face.

There was only one thing I remember distinctly—I wanted to talk about Jake the entire dinner, but I never did because I didn't want them to think I was focusing on it. But I was, completely.

At this point, I didn't know what to do. Compared to before, when I was driven to do something for Jake, at this point I just wanted to escape from his memory—and it haunted me. It haunted my dreams, my daydreams, my thoughts—and minute details were smothering me as they came back. Finally, after 10 months, the shock was beginning to wear off, and I could feel myself finally understanding what had happened. That no matter what I did, he would not be coming back. That he would never be coming back. That these memories I had—they're not shared anymore. While I had thought about it before, I was beginning to process this now. I wondered if I had been doing the right thing.

Instead of driven, I felt guilty. I felt guilty that I felt this way. It's not that his memory was becoming a burden—that would have almost been better. His memory was something I was actively trying to avoid, to suppress. That felt worse.

"I was talking about The Grog Shop with my coworkers, and they said it's a cool place. When did you want to leave again? When's the

show?" Jimmy asked as he took a sip of his Moscow mule. Immediately I wondered if this was a good idea or not. I already was feeling buzzed, and I could feel my thoughts escaping me, away from this moment. Escaping to the past, again. I knew I could trust him. I still do trust him. But I did not want him to worry. I wanted to be happy. I wanted him to be happy.

I had found it difficult to plan things with people because at this point, I knew I could not predict where my mind would be at any given time. This was even more difficult when I was just visiting someone, when everything was so intricately planned out beforehand. When it was planned, my mind was somewhat leveled. It wasn't leveled now.

I had already bought the tickets. I had already told them this is what we would be doing tonight. This was the first time I was really hanging out with Jimmy since seeing him at Jake's funeral. I wanted it to be a good time, a better time.

"Let's leave at eight," I said.

***

I could feel my two worlds colliding the moment I entered the venue. I knew I had been a different person than I truly was at these shows, and I knew my brother would be able to tell, of all people. I fumbled through my purse to find my ID and showed it to the bouncer, and he let Jimmy and me in. Katie had bought her own ticket. (Sorry I didn't buy you one, Katie. That was thoughtless.) She followed us into the venue. I asked Jimmy and Katie what they wanted to drink and went straight to the bar.

In front of me, a couple. The woman was sitting on the man's lap. Instead of thinking they looked happy together, I assumed that what they were doing was fake, mocking. I pushed behind his back and ordered my drink. I'm not sure if they noticed. In retrospect, I hope they didn't. What they were doing wasn't wrong. What I was doing was wrong.

I grabbed our three drinks. Jimmy and Katie were standing near the merch stand. I walked toward them.

Next to them, there was a young guy, early 20s, talking my brother's ear off about something he had never heard of and had no interest in. Something about some local stoner metal band he had seen two weeks ago. My brother shifted his weight back and forth, deviated his eyes around the room, as the kid continued to talk about the crowd, the amps, the effects. Everything. I could tell Katie wanted to escape the conversation before the kid directed his attention toward her.

"I just have to grab something for a friend quick. I'll be right back," I said.

"I'll go with you," Katie said. She followed me to the merch stand as I composed my thoughts.

This time, I didn't need to plan any justification to be there. Petrina, my friend from the Madison concert, had asked if I could get her one of their tapestries. This was my mission for this concert. I fumbled through my thoughts as I thought about juggling the two worlds—my personal life, and, for lack of a better term, my stage persona. These two worlds did not intersect, not even a little, and I had made sure to keep it that way. Until now.

This time, at the merch stand, I put on a different mask—one that didn't fit quite right. One that I thought would mesh the real and the fabricated together. One where I had my shit together. No bullshit.

"We're out of tapestries," the drummer, Robby, said. "Sold out." I froze for a second, plan foiled, then shifted.

"Bummer. But listen, though. My friend said she wants a tapestry. I can't go home empty-handed. She'd kill me." (This was a lie. Petrina would kill me if I told her I made a stink about it.)

"What would be the next best thing?" I asked.

He looked at me for a second, to gauge whether I was being serious. I feigned my best serious, no-bullshit face.

"Well, the sticker is similar, I guess. I guess you could get her one of those?" He paused. I looked at him. He looked at me. A moment of silence.

"Okay, I'll take one sticker, please." I handed him $3, then talked with him for a second about how I appreciated his art. He was the one who designed their merch, and it had a unique feel to it. I wanted to tell him that. Once we were done, Katie and I walked back to Jimmy, who was still listening to the guy who was talking with him before. He was still talking about the same band.

I stepped in. "I've never heard of that band. Tell me more." I tried, but he was already laser-focused on telling my brother all about this band. I continued to try to save my brother, but this kid would not relent. Finally, Jimmy had enough.

"I'm going to get another drink. You want anything?" he said. "Definitely. I'm coming with you," said Katie. Understandable.

The kid shifted his focus to me as soon as my brother left. "I just turned 21 last week, so this is the first time I can go to this place. Good timing, huh?" he told me. I understood where this kid was coming from. He was there alone, presumably his first show alone.

Before I could add anything, he delved into a story about how he had snuck into venues before but it felt good to be "actually, legit here."

What is this, New Orleans? I thought.

"Hey, listen, when they come back, tell them I'll be right back," I told him. And even though I felt bad leaving him alone, I figured it'd be good for him in the long-run. Character-building. For a minute, I wondered if I was just like that guy in St. Louis, who had asked me why I was traveling and then left abruptly when I said too much. I decided I didn't care. *He'll figure it out*, I justified.

I went back to the merch stand and fumbled up a reason to return.

"My friend, Petrina—she's never going to believe me that there are no tapestries. Could you write her a note, then sign it?" Again, he looked at me, expecting it to be a joke, but I gave him my best no-bullshit face. I told him her name, and even though I noticed he spelled it wrong, I didn't correct him. We talked about her name and I pulled "it's Greek" out of my ass, to have a quick answer. It seemed right. (It's not—sorry,

Robby. It's Norwegian.) I made small talk about how I had seen the band in a few other cities, and that they always put on a good show.

I didn't see the lead singer, Parks, sitting in back until he said, "Hello, Becky." And for a second, I panicked before I processed that it was him—that he had a reason to know my name, that he wasn't a complete stranger.

Again, it was difficult to start all over again completely when I was following the same people around, no matter how hard I tried. No matter how many masks I wore. I had never talked with the drummer, so he didn't know me. It was easy to start over with him, to be just another face. Because Parks knew my face, I was no longer anonymous.

"Good luck. I'm sure you guys will do great tonight!" I said to Parks. "We'll try, but no promises."

I said, without thought, without thinking about how it might come off, "Parks, my family is here. Don't fuck with my family." Ineloquently. Again, this no-bullshit, no-nonsense mask didn't fit me well—it hung awkwardly. If anything, it didn't make any sense. A disconnect from what was actually happening. A disconnect from the normal and the real.

Before I could process this, I saw Jimmy and Katie with three IPAs, overflowing, so I wished Parks and Robby good luck before returning to my family. As the kid I had abandoned talked at my brother some more, I stared at the wall. I thought about how rude I had been toward Parks until the opener started. I made my way to the front, by the speakers, and Katie followed me.

Handsome Jack opened, a band from Lockport, New York. Bluesy. Fun. Easy to sing along without knowing the lyrics. The crowd loved them, and went crazy for them. I tried to stay at the periphery, near the sound blasting out of the speakers.

I remember Katie trying to say something, but I couldn't hear her. I'm guessing it was something like, "I'm going to stand away from these blasting speakers because I like my hearing", because she walked away

when she was done talking. I looked over to Jimmy and he was still standing by the kid, who was head-banging a little too aggressively. Jimmy leaned up against a post, beer in hand.

I hope he's having fun, I thought. *I hope they're having a good time.*

I wondered if I should stand by them, but decided against it. I knew I wanted to be alone now.

I was no longer thinking *Where's Jake?* Now, I thought, *Damn, I wish Jake was here*. No matter how angry we were with each other, concerts were where we were able to reconnect. I guess kind of like how some couples have makeup sex after a fight, concerts had always been our makeup sex.

The last music festival Jake and I went to was Open Air Chicago. Summer 2016. July. Rammstein was headlining that night. And the reason I didn't fully consider this the last concert is because it wasn't that. It was a spectacle. It was the performance that drew me in, not the music. Plus, I knew they wouldn't be on a U.S. tour again anytime soon, and even if they were, there was no way I could afford to follow them.

At the time of the festival, Jake and I were both living in Madison. He was studying law, and he one of two people in the program chosen for a full ride, which included working with a professor on a case. I was working full-time and dealing with a very stressful car theft fiasco, as well as a few creative side projects.

The day of the festival, we were both stressed and overworked, and we both took it out on each other. I told him the wrong directions. I forgot to put his laundry in the dryer. His shirt was musty. He wouldn't share his breakfast sandwich. We fought. Because we were both not in our heads, we said everything. We cut. But the moment we were there, at the concert, he put his arm around me and kissed me. I knew everything would be okay.

Now, June 10, 2017, nearly one year later, I looked around to see if there was anyone who looked remotely like him—not to act on it, but to pretend that just for that night, he was out there having fun. I was

searching for someone to look at and to pretend, but there was no one. I tried to get lost in the music, but like I had been earlier 2017, I felt myself falling again. Each memory kicked me in the gut. Each wave of guilt tugged tears from my eyes, and I tried my best to keep them from falling. I put on my tough mask again and sang along, eyes shut.

***

Even after we got home, as I laid in bed, exhausted, I couldn't escape the thoughts that had been haunting me for the past month. The negative. The traumatic. I tried to think of anything else, anything, but my mind deviated to our trip to Belgium, when we went to Rock Werchter, when I first noticed that something wasn't quite right.

We had been apart for six months—he was living in Germany, and I was living in the United States and in Spain. Once we reunited, I noticed his dramatic mood shifts were more pronounced and more extreme than before. I could tell he was trying to control them, but it was a struggle. I felt the tension, but I didn't know how to address it.

I had been too stuck in my head at that time in the most self-loathing way. I assumed he was mad at me, and I assumed his hate-filled words were justified. And I saw that he felt guilty later. I saw that he regretted everything he said.

In these arguments, I assumed I was doing something wrong. I usually found out he was right, in the end. In the past, we used to argue, but we were always able to come to some sort of logical conclusion—which ended up with him being right in the end. And while this sounds like he demeaned me, this wasn't the case, at all. Not even close. He usually was right, in the end. He had a knack for that. He was blunt, but when he was in his right mind, his motives were true and selfless.

I convinced myself this must have been when he shifted, or at least the beginning. I convinced myself that, if I hadn't been so selfish at that time, I could have helped. I could have done something. Even in part.

I became obsessed with these moments. I became obsessed with what I could have done, knowing what I knew now. I became obsessed with what I didn't know, and what I would never know.

Chapter Four

I left my car parked at Jimmy and Katie's house and took a Greyhound to Pittsburgh a few days later, where All Them Witches would be playing two shows in a row. Again, I bought my tickets ahead of time, for both dates. I would be staying there from Wednesday night to Friday morning, and the shows were on Wednesday and Thursday.

Unlike St. Louis, this time, I focused on finding a place that had a yard. I wanted a place where I could go for a walk if I wanted to, and I found it—a place butting up to Frick Park with several paths I could get lost in if I wanted to. A place to go outside of the room I would be staying in, where I could still be alone without getting stuck in my head, as I had in St. Louis.

This time, I took off work, and planned all of the fun things I would do before the trip. I looked on *Atlas Obscura*, which I used as my travel guide, and found a few things: Conflict Kitchen, a restaurant that only served food from countries that the United States is in conflict with; Randyland, a notable section of street covered in beautiful art made from scraps and rubble; The Center for PostNatural History; and other things.

However, as I discovered in Cleveland, my mind was different now. I ditched all plans completely as soon as I learned that Conflict Kitchen

had closed down the month before. This was my excuse to cancel all of the plans I had made before.

I worked the morning from my brother's house, then boarded the Greyhound around 2:00 pm. I would get to Pittsburgh around 4:00 pm, which gave me plenty of time to settle in before the show that night. I had packed my own food, so I didn't plan on going out to eat that night. I was eating more now, and even though it wasn't great (mostly peanut butter toast), at least it was something.

I got on the bus, took the first window seat available, and put my headphones in immediately. I played Valerie June, followed by Rush, then back to Valerie June as I waited for the rest of the passengers to board. A man sat down next to me, introduced himself, and shook my hand.

Oh boy, my head is not here right now, I thought, but as always, I focused on focusing my eyes and my mind outward. My two masks—I felt as if I had packed them in my bag, which was below us now, in cargo. I put on a new one, one of the nice girl who was just going on a fun, definitely not emotionally-loaded trip for the week.

No negative emotion here, none at all, I thought. I tried to say this with a fake, overly enthusiastic smile.

I learned that he was an entrepreneur from London, and that he was traveling across the United States to meet with clients. He went to Pittsburgh often because one of his major clients was there. I asked him what there was to do there, and he gave me a few suggestions—all way above my price range.

I could tell the conversation was fizzling, so I told him I wanted to take a nap before I got there. To be honest, I just wanted to listen to my music and to turn my brain off as best I could. I put on more Valerie June—this time, "Love You Once Made," and noted how all nostalgic love songs now reminded me of Jake's death. Because this had been my first true breakup, if you could call it that, I wondered if this was how all breakups felt. I half-jokingly decided I didn't ever want to date, knowing I wouldn't be able to go through this again. This happened with most love songs I listened to lately—not that it hurt so much anymore (oddly, it didn't) but it was a change in perspective.

When Jake and I first started dating, he sang a Coldplay song to me while we were exploring a quarry. Under a sky of shooting stars, he sang "Green Eyes" to me. Coldplay—the first concert we went to, with his brother, Max, and Max's girlfriend at the time. Neither of us knew Coldplay, but we both loved concerts, and we had free tickets. This was the first time I told him that I loved him, as paper butterflies spewed out from the stage and into the crowd. We were 17, then.

At the quarry, after he sang to me, it took me a full half-hour to get the courage to correct him—that my eyes were blue, not green, but that I didn't care, and that I still loved when he sang to me. I remember I ruined my pair of shoes that night, tumbling down a steep hill of rocks. I remember there was a meteor shower.

I remember we stayed out until sunrise, but I can't remember what we talked about. I tried to think back, but it was gone. I couldn't remember.

Then, I felt a tap on my shoulder. The man next to me was holding out his earbud. "Here, listen to this. This is music from my country." And even though he said he was from London, I could tell he had Indian roots. It was something like electronica Bollywood, mixed with guitar. I didn't know what to think of it. I didn't hate it. Just not my thing.

"Oh wow. That's unique!" I said as I handed him the earbud back.

"No, keep listening. This is where it gets good," he said, with one brow raised, as if he was revealing a secret. To be honest, it sounded exactly the same as before, as if he had restarted the song. *Maybe I'm only hearing half of the song. Maybe the good parts were in his earbud*, I justified.

"Pretty rock and roll, right?" he said.

"Yeah, it's interesting!" I said. "I think I'm going to go back to sleep now, though, but thanks!"

I closed my eyes, and even though I felt him tap my shoulder again, I pretended I was asleep. For whatever reason, this faux-leather jacket I bought used on eBay, one I wore for most of my trip, made people think I was a lot more rock and roll than I really was. This wasn't the first time someone made that assumption. I wish it had come

with a disclaimer. *Maybe that's why someone was selling it for so cheap*, I thought. "This jacket comes with an attitude that you may or may not prescribe to," the description should have said.

My mind deviated to what I didn't know once more, back to the quarry.

But what had Jake said? I thought.

Finally, I got to Pittsburgh, and it was raining harder than it had been in St. Louis. *Flood warnings*, and *possible hail*, I heard as soon as I stepped off the bus. And it did hail. Almost as soon as I walked out of the Greyhound station, it started to hail, then let up almost as quickly as it started.

The man next to me in the Greyhound offered to buy me Subway, but I said, "No, thank you." He asked what I would be doing that night, and I told him I was going to see a concert. When he asked for what band, I told him it was sold out. I wasn't sure if it actually was, but it was a fair assumption.

Once I started talking with people, it was like breaking a seal, even if I didn't necessarily connect with that first person. Once I started talking with people, I didn't want to stop. As I reached out, I was able to push aside my negative emotions—the ones that had haunted me only a day before.

Once the negative emotions were compacted to the back of my mind, I felt I needed to fill that space with something new. New connections. New conversations. Even if the first connection hadn't worked, I didn't want to stop trying. This restarted every day. If I connected with one person, I spent the rest of the day trying to make more connections, even if they were only surface level. If I didn't connect on a particular day, those previously compacted negative memories spread into the void and haunted me.

After the man from London walked off, I ordered a Lyft.

When I got into the Lyft—a silver, beat-up Chrysler—I stepped between two empty Big Gulp cups before buckling myself in. All I could smell was cigarette smoke. I looked to my driver—she was drinking a Big Gulp, a half-burned cigarette in her mouth. Windows up. Ed Hardy pads on her seats.

I wanted to ask if it was even okay to smoke in your car if you're the driver, but quickly stopped myself. *That would be rude*, I thought. Plus, I didn't really care. Coming from Milwaukee, which had been one of the last cities to ban smoking in public places, it reminded me of childhood, in a strange Pittsburgh-ian way.

"So, where are you going? Where is this?" She asked me before I could even greet her.

"I'm staying at a house east of here, in Regent Square." "Where in Regent Square?"

"I'm not from here. It's my first time, so I'm not entirely sure. If you want, I can look it up, but the directions your GPS will give will be better than any I can give."

She sighed. Not a good start. I tried to recover the conversation. *Focus outward.*

"Crazy storm we're having, huh?" I said.

"Yep," she said, cigarette dangling from her mouth. She blew the smoke over her left shoulder. It started raining harder, hail cracking under her tires. She turned her wipers on high, which is when I noticed one was only half a wiper. Luckily, it was on my side, not hers. I wondered how the hell she got 4.7 stars, and I wondered what the other drivers would be like, but I corrected myself. *Maybe I'm judging too quickly*, I thought. *I'm probably no five-star passenger right now either*, I thought.

No music was playing—only the sound of rain hitting the windows and wipers squeaking on high.

She finished her cigarette and put it out in the cup holder next to me, which she had turned into a makeshift ashtray. We got on the highway.

"These streets always seem to flood for some reason. The water always sits on the road. Swear to God, every time we get rain, there's a flood," she said to the outside air.

"Flat roads, maybe?" I said, suddenly escaping my mind again to connect.

"Beg your pardon?"

"Usually, they're curved slightly so rain doesn't sit on them. It's nothing. Nevermind."

It started hailing again—but when I looked on the other side of the road, it wasn't hailing.

"It always seems to hail on this side of the street, never on that side. Never understood why," she said again, to the air.

"That's so strange! I've never seen that!" And this was legitimate. While it was raining on one side of the highway, it was hailing on the other. I could see it traveling toward us, until it was pounding on her windshield, as we hit a dead stop.

This didn't seem to completely clear the air, but it at least constructed a bridge over the rift from before. I asked her if she was originally from Pittsburgh, and she said, "Yes, all my life."

Past this, we talked about her daughter—she going to college in September on a scholarship. How proud she was of her. "A prodigy," she said. Then, she shifted focus to her long-time boyfriend, who in her words "wasn't the best," which she said with a shrug. He was distant, and the love had gone stale. "But at least he's a good support system," she justified, then dropped it, so I figured it was something she didn't want to talk about. Just something she wanted to address.

There was a minute of silence before she said, "Wow, this rain will not let up," as she coughed, then lit up another cigarette.

We talked about how she was trying to quit smoking, which is when I told her I had recently quit snus (I had, even though I still carried my tin with me, in some sort of strange challenge to myself). I told her a story about my grandma, who had smoked a pack a day for 70 years until one day, she quit cold turkey. Until the day she was moved to assisted living, which was five years after she quit, she still had a full pack of "emergency cigarettes" in her medicine cabinet. She never touched a single one. At least, not to my knowledge, and certainly not from her emergency pack.

We talked about why I was here, which is when I told her, suddenly, very briefly, of what I was actually doing—that after my boyfriend died, I went on a manic trip following around the last band we saw together. I told her that at each concert, I was buying a ticket for him, then giving it away to a stranger.

This was the first time I truly said it out loud in full. To be honest, it caught me by surprise at how quickly it came out.

"That's sweet," she said. "I guess," I said.

My mind hung on this. How great it felt to release this thought, and to have a quick answer back. A quick validation. A quick acceptance. Instead of filling my head with new information about new people and new places, instead of covering up what I was doing with facades and fabrications, I made even more room once I had said this simple sentence out loud. To me, after it had been spiraling in my head for so long—especially the doubt—it felt euphoric to finally release what I was doing. To release what had happened.

"Well, here it is. Your place. Have fun at that concert tonight! Stay safe!"

"You too!" I said, and I realized my words didn't make any sense in this context. I tried to smile it away as I shut the door, and waved goodbye.

I imagined the first time I'd tell the story of my trip, it would be more profound. But, like most things in life, the things you build up the most will most likely end up being the most uneventful. Mostly because you build them up to some inhuman, unrealistic level of importance. To have it brushed off so cleanly felt like I was doing the right thing—that, if anything, at least it was "sweet." If it had been built up more, I feel like I would have felt more uncomfortable. More fake. Less profound.

***

I looked at the clock, and it was now 5:00 pm. The drive that should have taken 20 minutes took an hour because of the weather. I had two hours to clean myself up, make my peanut butter toast, and head out

to the show. I spent most of it reading a Pittsburgh guide book my host had left and watching the rain pour before I decided to run into the shower and change. This time, I had not planned a distraction. This time, I didn't even feel the need to put on a mask. I didn't want to fake it anymore. I wanted to connect, *legitimately* connect. With anyone.

I took another Lyft. By now, the weather had cleared, but hail still crunched underneath the car's tires. On this drive, we talked about the Penguins game against the Predators. The Penguins had won the Stanley Cup. He told me about some sports commentator he followed, then pulled up a few sound clips of things the commentator had said. The driver laughed, but I didn't get it because I don't follow sports. I laughed along anyway. It felt good to be happy, even if it was superficial. I felt clear, and laughter came easily.

I got there when the doors opened, and I told the bouncer to give one ticket away, as usual. He told me that it was a sold-out show, so this would be much appreciated. I didn't think much about it when he told me—didn't think to tell him not to tell anyone.

At the bar, I saw there was a specific menu option for a random drink, based on your favorite drink. I told her I wanted something like a gin and tonic, but not as alcoholic. She made me something. We talked for a minute before it got too busy—about the venue, about the bands, about the weather.

Suddenly, a man—younger, shaggy blonde hair, wide-eyed—surprised me by shaking one of my shoulders.

"THANK YOU!" he said. "THANK YOU SO FUCKING MUCH!"

And I didn't know what was happening, so gut-punch impulse, I turned to him and said, "You're welcome, but for what?"

"For the ticket. Thank you!" And at this moment I thought, *Fuck, I forgot to tell the bouncer not to tell*. I tried to push that thought to the back of my brain so it didn't appear in my eyes.

"Oh, yeah, that. No big. Not a prob." I tried to shrug it off, so as to show it wasn't as profound to me as it really was.

"Seriously, my friends all got tickets, and when I tried to buy tickets, maybe 20 minutes later, they were all sold out. You saved my ass, man! You saved it!" For a second, he held my shoulder before saying, "Want a drink? What can I get you?"

And I get where he was coming from—had someone given me a free ticket to a sold-out show, I probably would have done the exact thing he was doing now, if not more. But at this point, as much as I wanted to connect, I did not want it to be overblown as I felt it was now. I felt that if I were to tell him why I was giving the ticket away, this would ruin the moment. Or, if anything, it would turn into something that it wasn't. The perspective would shift. I didn't want to do that. Again, this was my burden to bare—not his. By receiving my free ticket, he was simply a vessel for my recovery.

And though I didn't want to connect in this way, I knew that, and given I wasn't being entirely responsible with my money, saving money anywhere would be pretty sweet. *If anything, if I were in his shoes, I would want to give the giver something in return, to be even*, I justified.

"Actually, a gin and tonic would be great," I told him. I got my drink, then he ordered me a gin and tonic. After I got my drink, he went to go visit his friends after giving me a hug a little too long for comfort. "THIS IS THE GIRL WHO GAVE ME HER TICKET!" he shouted to his friends, and they all gave me an enthusiastic thumbs up.

I was grateful he didn't ask me why. I wanted these connections to be on my own terms. I was okay with opening up on my own terms. I was not ready for someone to pry.

"What was that about?" the bartender asked.

"Don't worry about it. Just something I've been doing in a few cities," I told her.

She dropped it, we made superficial small talk, and as it got busier she went to help someone else.

***

Handsome Jack was still opening, so I listened to them again. I connected with the same songs differently this time. Again, as I was touring around, any sort of similarities became homes, connections. I listened to them play, and I sang along to the parts I knew. Same words, new context. One guy put his arm around my shoulders and his friend's shoulders and we shouted along to one of their songs: "Take me back home take me way back home, take me back home to sleep!" At this point, I was still holding two drinks in my hand, spilling a lot of both everywhere.

He kissed my cheek at the end of the song, then immediately apologized and said he got caught up in the moment. I said it was cool, and moved forward. This was also not the kind of connection I wanted. I felt vulnerable—felt the need to retreat into myself again—but I stopped myself as best I could. I finished one of my drinks, then walked toward the bar to set one of my glasses down. It was intermission, and people were walking around and talking.

I started talking with a woman and her husband, both early 40s. The kind of couple that you can tell has been together for so long that they start to look like each other, even if it's just their mannerisms—the knowing side-glances that lasted milliseconds, the kind you'd miss if you'd blink at the wrong time. I don't remember their names, so I'll call them Cheryl and Steve.

They didn't know the bands playing, but had heard they'd be good, so they decided to swing by. They knew the bartender, so we all talked about the band as she refilled their drinks.

Steve was in a metal band, and Cheryl worked at a bar downtown. They had lived in Pittsburgh most of their lives, but like me, they tried to travel as much as they could. We talked about the different cities they had been to, and I talked about the cities I had been to. "There's no real reason to move if where you're living is affordable enough to travel. Just use it as your hub," they told me.

I wanted to say, "But I need to find my hub. Milwaukee is not my hub anymore."

But their friend came up to us at that moment—also early 40s, with short, black hair teased into a ponytail. I couldn't tell if it was intentional, or if she hadn't time to brush her hair, or maybe she had been head-banging too hard. I don't remember her name, either, so for clarity's sake, I'll call her Stephanie. Stephanie told us she'd be going toward the front, two drinks already in hand. All Them Witches was setting up.

I noticed my second drink was mostly empty (mostly from spilling it during Handsome Jack), so I ordered a PBR. I felt myself going back momentarily to Madison, when I rushed to the bar after my gin to get a PBR just to emulate Jake.

At this point, I told myself I was getting a PBR on my own terms. As much as I loved Jake, I knew that my need to connect and to move forward was greater than my need to perpetuate this honorary ritual I had crafted. But because we had been together for so long, I didn't know what to do without him. While this had been his thing, the longer we were together, it started to become "our" thing as our personalities grew closer with time.

Now, he wasn't here. I sipped my PBR. *Now, it's my thing, I guess*, I thought, nostalgic but absent.

I acknowledged I was alone now. Fully. My pain was aching, not desperate. I was able to fill this hole with new connections, new memories—while still retaining, for the most part, the memories I had with him. I tried to focus on forgetting the negative. To keep those memories that made me happy, peaceful. This is what I was trying to do. This was my goal.

All Them Witches started playing, and Stephanie, now in front, started singing along and screaming, "WOO!", which contrasted everyone else, who were pretty chill. Two guys in front of me started mocking her, and I told them to knock it the fuck off, with a bit too much bite in my words.

"What, do you know her?"

"No, but if she's having fun, that's not your problem. You do you. Don't judge other people."

And again, this was a different version of my St. Louis self. Instead of actively making people feel better, I wanted to make sure everyone else also treated others with respect. The kind of hero nobody wanted or needed. I realized she was perfectly comfortable with herself and didn't need me to stand up for her, but I felt it was necessary. I was lucky they didn't say anything back to me. They just moved forward, a raised brow side-glance to each other.

This is something Jake used to do. Another trait that had started out as his, but the longer we knew each other, became "ours." Kind of like how a couple starts to look similar the longer they're together, like Cheryl and Steve.

This was something I always admired about Jake—how willing he was to stand up for people, even if it made him look like a jackass. A global view, instead of self-centered. Now, alone, I had mixed feelings on being the person to carry this on. Again, I acknowledged that I was my own person now, but I also realized he was no longer here to perpetuate those great traits he had. Those he shared with me, those he influenced me with. I admired them. Now, I felt there was a void. He was no longer around to do this. In a strange way, I felt proud that I could keep this going for him. As tough as he tried to act, I know that in his heart, he, too, just wanted people to be accepting, to be open. To be true.

If anything, it felt better than concentrating on the negative, as I had been doing only a day before. In retrospect, it's possible because I was now in a new place, where I didn't know anyone. Where I was forced to take everything in and to learn my surroundings as I explored them. I could feel my mentality shifting again. I could feel my mind actively trying to recover. Instead of simply actively focusing my eyes outward, I tried to focus on forward motion. Making sure my mind was also connecting. I tried to focus on the positive.

***

I finished my PBR and ordered another one. I told the bartender to close me out, and sipped on my beer. I tried to make it last the entire

set, which I almost did until the last song, where I chugged the rest of it and set it on the bar. I went to the bathroom and passed Handsome Jack on my way. I told them they did great. They were thankful. When I left the bathroom, All Them Witches was playing their encore, and where people had been more spread out, they were now compact, each trying to get closer to the stage than they had been before.

I stood near the periphery and saw Cheryl and Steve. They said they would be going to Jack's after the show, right next door, and I said I'd meet them there. "It's nothing fancy—you could probably find a hipper bar down the street," they said, and I told them it was fine, that I wasn't that fancy.

All Them Witches ended, and the place was beginning to clear already as they were packing up their gear. The general consensus was, "Holy shit, that was great." Some people hung around to tell the band they did great, so I decided to stick around to do the same.

Stephanie came up to us and said, "HOLY SHIT!" Cheryl laughed, and said she was their "crazy friend."

"Just because I like to have a good time doesn't mean I'm *crazy*," Stephanie said, looking at me for validation.

The young, hip one, supposedly. I agreed with her. Mostly because I didn't know what to say.

Then suddenly, from behind me, I heard, "HOLY SHIT THANK YOU OH MY GOD!" It was my friend from before, the guy who had gotten my free ticket, grabbing both of my shoulders.

"THAT WAS SO FUCKING GOOD!" he said as he shook my body. "I CAN NEVER REPAY YOU ENOUGH! HOLY SHIT!"

Again, I said, "Not a problem. Anytime. You don't have to repay me. I like to do that kind of thing." Trying to regain my balance again. After being literally shook on heels, after a few drinks, that was difficult. But I managed.

"No, you have NO IDEA! THAT WAS FUCKING AMAZING!"

And while I wanted to say, "I was there too, I know!" I decided to say, "Honestly, not a problem." I gave him my best impression of a genuine smile. Again, while what he was doing wasn't totally abnormal, to me, it felt uncomfortable to acknowledge the person I had given the ticket to. Especially since he was so different from Jake, or at least my memory of Jake. I tried to push this to the back of my mind again, to keep this from showing in my eyes.

He told me he would be going to some bar down the street, with moose heads on the wall, and he said if I wanted a shot I should go there. I said, "No, thanks." I told him I already had plans with my friends. He thanked me again before running after his friends, who were threatening to leave without him.

"Wow, you've got some serious game," Stephanie said. "We're going to find you someone tonight, for sure."

In my head I said, *Please God, no thank you*, but outwardly I said, "That's not why I'm here," and I looked away.

I found it difficult to address the no-mask persona in these situations. I found it difficult how much information was too much information, how little was too little. I knew I needed to be direct—that I was in no place to be "hooked up" and to be honest, I probably never would be, no matter my mentality. No matter my past experiences. I found it easiest to divert instead. This was something I had struggled with in the past—my directness. I'm naturally a people-pleaser. However, now I realized if I ignored my need for recovery and went along with what other people wanted me to do, this would hurt me more. I needed to protect myself. Without my mask.

I planned on asking the band if they would give my ticket away anyway, so I lingered back. I wanted to avoid, at all costs, another episode like tonight, where the person found out I gave it away and felt the need to repay me.

I saw the band was standing in the middle of the room, looking at their equipment, which they kept up for the next night's show. I walked up to them with a $20 bill in hand, then stood next to Allan.

"Here. Use this to buy someone a ticket tomorrow. Don't tell them it was me," I said. I tried to be discreet, but with house music still blasting from the speakers, my whisper came out as a shout. Robby looked at me with a raised brow, then looked away.

Allan looked at me. Paused. "Wait, excuse me, what?" And for a moment, I could tell he didn't remember me, until he did. But only briefly. By face, but definitely not by name or from where.

"Sorry, I didn't explain that well. Would you please keep that $20, then just let someone in for free tomorrow? Buy someone's way in?"

"I mean, I guess I can do that, but are you sure?" he said as he took the bill, looking from the bill to me.

"100%," I said, avoiding eye contact. "...But why?"

"Listen, I gotta go. I'm going to the bar next door. Thanks. I appreciate it!" Again, this no-mask persona was difficult. It felt good to be my true self again, to interact with people without a mask blocking my vision, but I felt it difficult emerging into the world while still being 100% honest. I'd rather divert than be wholly honest, no matter how badly I wanted to say why I was here. No matter how badly I wanted to make more room in my mind for more experiences.

Instead of opening up, I left.

***

"Want a cigarette?" Cheryl asked, and even though I didn't smoke and was trying to quit snus I said, "Sure."

She pulled out a pack of Marlboro Reds and gave me one. I remembered what Jake said, that *you look crazy standing around without a cigarette*. I wanted to appear as sane as possible. Without my mask, I felt exposed. I said, "Thank you."

Parks was outside, and I felt a strange wave of "I need to apologize for everything I did before, when I was not feeling right," though I acknowledged the chances he remembered half of it was slim to none.

It bothered me as I smoked my cigarette—to acknowledge what I had been doing was crazy, to apologize for any inconveniences I caused them. To let them know I wasn't trying to inconvenience them. That I appreciated what they were doing. That I wasn't trying to patronize them. That I wanted to treat them as human beings. In retrospect, this was probably a manifestation of my connection fixation. I needed to connect, on a real human level, but I didn't know how to do it yet.

We walked toward the bar. I turned around. I put out my cigarette. I walked toward Parks.

And even as I was walking toward him and actively concentrating on keeping my mask off, I could feel it creeping back on again. While it was easier to forge new connections now, it was difficult for me to reconnect with people I had met before as my newly unmasked self.

Instead of focusing my mind outward as I had been trying to do, I found I could only focus my eyes outward. My mind still stayed locked, no matter how much I tried to coax it out, no matter how much alcohol I had in my system.

"Hey, I just wanted to apologize for being so rude in Cleveland. I meant it as a joke, but it didn't come off that way. Wanted to let you know I didn't mean anything by it," I said, my eyes focused on the pavement, lost behind my hand gestures, as if I was giving a speech rather than talking with one person.

"I don't remember you being rude." He paused, in thought, then said, "Wait, what did you say?" He was sipping on something in a coffee cup, one brow raised.

"I told you to not fuck with my family," I said, finally making eye contact. He laughed, and I tried to laugh with. Dynamic conversation was difficult from behind my mask. I was only good at preplanned conversations, which is why I had planned reasons to be there before (card, notebook, etc.) In those conversations, I felt relatively in control. Now, I found myself empty-handed. I fumbled.

"Oh. Hah. Well, I didn't hear it," he said, and while I expected the conversation to end there, he then asked, "So, why are you here again? You seem to be everywhere."

I froze for a second—and for a minute, I considered telling him—but in the final seconds, I convinced myself that if he knew the reason, it would ruin his night, or he would feel the need to console me. It was the last thing I needed, and I didn't want to inconvenience further. I felt the honest reason would be another imposition I'd put them at.

Again, the egocentricity reappeared, and in my head, I imagined that if I released my problems to the world, they would cause the same amount of pain to everyone who heard it—that my problems would be the center of everyone's world if I released them.

"I work remotely, so I figured this would be a good way to take advantage of that. A good way to see the country," I said. I changed the subject before he could implore further. "Is that coffee you're drinking?"

"Jack and Coke," he said.

"Oh," I said. "Cool." I paused, shifted my weight, and looked around the corner. "Well, I gotta go. I have some mom-friends waiting for me at Jack's. I'll see you tomorrow. Have a good night!" *Mom-friends*. I kicked myself a little. Another inauthentic and inaccurate joke from behind the mask.

"Y-you too!" he said as he walked back into the venue.

***

I walked back toward Jack's, where I found my new friends sitting at the bar.

Before the concert, I had looked this bar up—the closest legitimate dive bar, according to Google, with a history. I had planned to come here anyway, but it felt good to know people here, even if I didn't know them that well.

"What do you want? We're paying," Stephanie said to me. "Something strong?"

I said it wasn't necessary, and that I just wanted to buy myself a beer, and that I had brought money for it. She said, "Fine."

"We're gonna find you someone tonight, though. Someone cute like you, which should be easy. We're gonna find you someone. Cute, single thing like you shouldn't be walking around here alone." She looked around the room, passing through every guy she saw.

And while I realized I hadn't said I was single, I guess it was a fair assumption. I had given them basic details before, like that I had been following the band alone. That I had been traveling across the Midwest, the South, and the East alone. That I would keep going after this.

I was about to say something, but Cheryl said, "That's her thing. She's a drunk matchmaker. If you want anyone, she'll make it happen."

And again, I tried to say something, but Steve said, "Jesus fucking Christ, settle down. We're just trying to have a good time. Maybe she just wants to hang—"

I looked up to all of them and blurted out, "I'm here because my boyfriend died. I don't want to be hooked up with anyone," suddenly. "I'm here because I found my boyfriend dead last year." I looked down at the bar, my heart pounding, and to keep myself from saying more I took a sip of my beer.

There was a silence, followed by, "Oh, holy shit." I saw the bartender from the corner of my eye, walking toward us, then turning on her heel as she read the situation from afar.

This isn't how I wanted it to come out. But it did. I tried to recover. I thanked the gods that the lighting was low as I felt tears welling in my eyes. Thankfully, none of them fell. They hung back, then reabsorbed.

"I'm okay. It's just that I'm not ready for that kind of thing yet." But as I feared, as soon as I let it out, it shifted the entire dynamic. *Now it's their burden, too*, I thought.

I took another drink of beer, and noticed it was already half gone. Now that they knew, I made a mental note to monitor myself. I didn't want them to worry about me more, didn't want them to think I was drinking my pain away. At this point, that's not what I was doing. At this point, I was trying to block out the immediate.

"Oh, honey," Cheryl said. "Honey. I'm so sorry. How did he pass?"

"Suicide," I said, as if I was ordering an Egg McMuffin, or sharing how my day was.

Every time I said "suicide," I couldn't help but picture finding him in my mind, a sliver of an image from behind a chain-locked door. *Thank Christ he thought to chain lock the door*, I thought again. I could only open it wide enough to see what I needed to see, to know what had happened.

I tried to keep this thought from appearing on my face. I tried to stay stoic. It wasn't a mask—it was repression. I guess a different kind of mask. A much more temporary mask, in retrospect. Much like the Marlboro I took from Cheryl earlier—something to cover up my immediate thoughts.

"Shit," Steve said. He shifted toward Stephanie. "Shit."

"It's cool," I assured him, one hand raised as if I was defending myself. "Don't worry about it. I just wanted to be honest. I didn't want to drag it out."

I looked at Stephanie. "We're cool. There's no way you could have known. It's cool."

I had another connection to my past, but this time, outside of my trip. A little over 10 months ago, at this point. The morning after I found Jake dead, I immediately agreed to inpatient treatment. Partly because I knew nobody knew what to do with me, and partly because I didn't know what to do with myself. When I got there, there were two sections—one for recovering addicts, one for mental health. I was in mental health, rightfully so. I was a wreck. Most people in my group were there for attempted suicide.

I didn't tell my story the first two days, until I did. Until I told everything. Until I told every detail, down to the bullet hole in the wall, down to how long he had been there, down to the last cryptic email he had sent me, which I admit now wouldn't have given me any sort of hint that he would do that but I had assumed at the time I should have seen it.

There was that same silence, until the group leader, a therapist, said, well intentioned, "Well, at least we can learn from Becky's story. At least we all still have our loved ones with us. Don't put your families through Becky's hardship."

At this moment, I felt just as alone as I had at that moment, as I had when I was sitting on a plastic chair in inpatient care. The statement "*At least we all still have our loved ones with us"* resonated in my head, and the implied *Now I have no one* filled my head again. I pushed it back.

Stephanie shifted her weight, then said, "Well, I think I'm going to go. I'm getting a call from someone, and this is getting a little heavy for me. I hope life treats you well, or, erm, at least better than before, Becky. I'll see you around." She backtracked out of the bar.

To be honest, I don't remember her phone ringing, but I don't blame her. I caught her off guard. That wasn't her fault. I didn't know how to process it, either. I couldn't blame her. I turned back to the bar, slouched, raising my shoulders in an attempt to retreat into myself physically. Trying to make myself smaller. Trying to disappear.

Cheryl held my arm for a second, and sighed. "Shit, you're too young for that." She looked to Steve, and their shared look was something I hadn't seen it before. Understanding. I felt that they understood what I was saying, exactly. I hadn't encountered this before. It was a connection—one far deeper than eye contact or surface-level interests.

"Five years ago, my brother committed suicide," she told me. I tried to make eye contact with her to say sorry, but I saw her eyes glued to the wood grains in the cherry-stained bar. I could tell that's not what she meant by telling me this. I could tell she didn't want sympathy. Like me, she just wanted to say it.

I remember explaining this to my friend the year before, a month after I found Jake. His neighbor had come over to his bonfire one night, uninvited, to tell him his grandson had been shot and died. After his neighbor told him about his grandson's death, he stood there for a moment, then walked away, as if he had invited them to a pig roast, emotionless.

I had told him that his neighbor probably just wanted to say it out loud, that he was still trying to process it, that he wanted to release it. I could relate to that, but this is the first time I actually encountered it from someone else.

"It's just, shit. I wouldn't wish that on anyone. You're too young for that," she said again.

"If it makes you feel better, it does get better," Steve said. She interrupted.

"No, it doesn't get better. It just gets different," she said. "I still think about him every day, but it's not the same as before. There will be a time when you're not running away from it, I can tell you that. There will be a time when you accept it, when you can settle down again. But that doesn't mean it gets easier." She took a sip of her beer. I could tell that, now, it was her turn to talk. I took a sip of my own beer, and waited for her to start again.

Instead, she asked me a question, though I could tell she wanted to say something else. She still had more to say, but she repressed it. She still did not look up from the bar. She was still lost in her thoughts.

"How's his family?"

"To be honest, outside of his mom and his older brother, they're not my biggest fans," I said. "I haven't talked with most of them since the funeral." I wanted to say that his mom probably only still talked with me because that was Jake's supposed dying wish. "Don't stop talking with Becky," he had told her the weekend before. In retrospect, it was probably partly that, but mostly because she is, simply put, an exceptionally selfless human being who truly wanted to be sure I was doing okay.

"You know, we felt the same way, about his wife. It's not about you. It's not about you at all. You knew him best. It's easy to use you as a scapegoat," she said. "It's easier to assume you knew something we didn't." And at this point, I felt like she wasn't talking with me at all—as if she was talking with someone else through me. Again, I could

relate to that. At this point, we were both saying things meant for other people, using the other person as a stand-in for someone else.

"I can understand it, though—we had gotten in a pretty terrible fight before, and—"

"No, it doesn't matter what you did. What you did was your choice. What he did—that was how he chose to deal with it. That's not your fault," she said. "But I'm not innocent. As I said, we did the same thing to my brother's wife. We still haven't talked with her, and it's been five years since he passed. I feel—"

"That's for the best," I said. "A clean break." And to be honest, I wasn't exactly sure if I meant that as I said it, but as it processed in my mind, I realized how accurate it really was. As much as the rejection hurt, it made it much easier to move on and try to build my own world again. Strangely, even right after it happened, I did not hate his family for it. I understood it. I'm grateful for that realization—that even though I was caught up in just about everything else, I wasn't caught up in that.

"Still though," she said. She looked at the bar again, then looked up to me. Connected again.

"Listen, my daughter works with trauma therapy. She's a volunteer. I'd really like you to meet her. I work at a bar downtown, and I can have her meet us tomorrow. I think you two would get along." I wrote down the name of her bar, and I said I'd let her know.

It was near midnight now, and they were closing out. Cheryl gave me a hug and told me she'd see me tomorrow. I told her I was happy to have met her, and I was looking forward to meeting her daughter the next day. I gave her husband a hug, too, and he wished me luck on my journey. I thanked them.

I still wasn't done. I walked down the street, to one of the bars they mentioned. Now that I had made a true connection, I felt addicted to the need to connect again. To find a deeper connection. A mental connection.

I sat down at one of the bars they recommended and realized I'd probably never connect with someone the same way here. I got sucked

into a conversation with someone who was there for a conference. For some reason, he immediately deviated to alien abduction stories. He was convinced that, two years ago, he had been abducted by an alien—and that, now, he wasn't his former self, but a hybrid alien. I listened and I asked questions, but when I noticed him leaning closer to me, I closed out and left abruptly.

I walked back to Jack's and talked with someone at that bar. Another escape. We noticed the security footage, dated pre-9/11 in the corner of the screen. We wondered if that was planned, or if that legitimately was there to try to make us feel safe, hoping we wouldn't look at the dates in the corner.

I looked for the note with the bar I had written down—Cheryl's bar. I couldn't find it. I must have dropped it somewhere. I asked the bartender if she knew where Cheryl worked and she said she had no idea. I asked for Cheryl's last name, and I'm pretty sure she thought I was trying to hit on her or creep on her, so the bartender wouldn't give me that information.

This was my biggest regret throughout the whole trip. I had made a connection, and I had screwed it up.

I left at bar close. I ordered another Lyft and made a mental note that I had to cool it on these trips. *Too expensive*, I thought.

Once my car arrived, I left. I fell asleep almost immediately, in the clothes I wore that night. Makeup still on. Purse underneath my arm. My mind was exhausted, my body ached.

Chapter Four (Continued)

I woke up with a massive hangover. I tried to will myself out of my bed, but I couldn't get up until 10:00 am.

Though the weather was nicer, I decided to work on a project I had brought with me. I was working on some flyers for a friend, one I would be staying with in New York City. A comedy show. I had all of my paper, my materials, and I worked on it for about 15 minutes before I got up again. Restless.

I have to do something manifested itself again. This time, it wasn't about Jake. It was a restless *I have to do something*, independent. For myself. I could feel myself regressing back, playing the night before over and over in my head. Replaying all the thoughts and the flashbacks I had.

I did Pilates. I made toast in the oven, then slathered too much peanut butter on it. Peanut butter everywhere. I cleaned up. I made more peanut butter toast, made another mess, then cleaned up again. I went for a quick walk in Frick Park, which butted up to the backyard of the place I was staying. The birds here were similar, yet different. Like a cover of a song I once loved but hadn't heard in a while. While I usually listen to music on my walks, it felt nice to just be outside, to listen to my surroundings.

But this was only momentary. *I've gotta get out of here*, I thought, about 20 minutes into my walk. *I have to connect. I can't get lost again*, I thought. I took a shower, then ordered another Lyft.

There had been a parade for the Pittsburgh Penguins that morning. As I found out on my drive the day before, they had won the Stanley Cup. According to this new Lyft driver, it had been a shit show. The parade broke a record for the loudest parade, or decibel level, according to him—but I never checked that fact, so don't take my word for it.

I was happy I wasn't there that morning.

All Them Witches was playing again that night, for the second night. I went near the same strip I had been the day before. I didn't want to deviate too far from that path. I walked further down the street I had

been on the night before. I found a comic book shop. It was something I had missed back in Cleveland, but I didn't realize it until I was here.

At first, the shop looked closed. All of the lights were off, and comics were stacked haphazardly in the window, but when I got in, I saw that this was only a very strange sort of decoration. Inside, the comics were neatly organized. I asked if there were any graphic novels, and he said, "No, strictly DC and Marvel. We also have some independent comics." I searched the independent section, but didn't find anything that caught my eye. To be fair, I was looking for something I knew. I wanted to reread something, but I found nothing I knew there. I thanked him, and left.

Further down the street was a sushi place, so I stopped in for some sushi. Cheap, but filling. I ordered a gin and tonic and watched the TV in front of me, at the bar. There was more on the Penguins, like flashbacks of their winning game and clips of the parade that morning (which, indeed, did look like a shit show).

Down the street, I got lost in a record shop. I talked with the owner, and he told me he had owned it for about 10 years. He told me it was fun to watch the clientele change—from "old fogies" like him to younger kids. I repeated something I heard before—that we liked the uncompressed sound, and that in digital copies, the sound was compressed. I told him this was why I liked going to concerts so much. He agreed.

Instead of buying music, I bought a Bukowski book. I remembered Jake had been reading *Ham on Rye* before he died, so I bought *Post Office*. I told myself this was for me, and that I had never read Bukowski's books, but I knew in the pit of my gut that this was me trying to extend a relationship that was now, literally, dead. I walked around the block, then walked around the block again. I thought about sitting and reading for a bit, but

I noticed nobody else was, so I didn't want to stick out. Instead, I chose to keep walking around the same block, black bag in hand.

I walked to the venue just as doors were opening. Because I still had two tickets, I immediately gave the extra ticket to someone behind me. In retrospect, I could have done this all along, but the need to

give it to someone random—that his ticket had gone to someone I didn't know—was an addiction. It kept me going. I could pretend his memory was in someone random. I couldn't pretend it was in someone I had made eye contact with, someone I had chosen. I didn't want to see the recipient, as I had the day before.

I pretended like it had been for someone who was supposed to be there, but bailed last second. He said he appreciated it, but didn't bring it up past that. I was grateful for that.

The same bartender I had talked with the night before was there again. We talked about the two bands, and she said she was excited to see them again. I agreed. I told her I wanted to order another take on a gin and tonic, and she gave it to me for free. I thanked her.

I heard one guy next to me talking about Handsome Jack, saying he hadn't heard anything by them, and I interrupted his conversation.

"They're great!" I told him. He looked a little taken back, and he introduced himself. I didn't know what else to say, so I deviated from there. I found more people to talk with. More connections.

I looked around for the people I had met last night—Cheryl, Steve, and Stephanie—but they weren't here. Everything seemed so superficial. And though I knew this was how connections worked when you traveled alone, you could never get to the heart of things right away with strangers, I still felt manic.

Again, I knew at this point I needed to connect on a mental level, as I had the night before. I felt the block coming back in my head. I felt the negative coming forward again. I felt the need to talk it out again, and the need was desperate. I saw Jake's eyes in my head. I wanted to block them out, too.

Handsome Jack started playing. I tried to move my way to the front. The guy in front of me was jumping around, and it was annoying me. When I tried to move past him, I said, "Excuse me." He turned around and said I was rude for pushing past him, and that I should have excused myself. I said I did. He told me he didn't hear me, so I pointed to the music blasting out of the speakers. "That's why," I told him.

This was rude, but I don't take it back. There are jerks everywhere you go. This was a constant. I had forgotten about this. *Not everyone is your friend*, I thought. *It's okay*, I thought. *Move past it*.

"Take me back home take me way back home, take me back home to sleep!" played again, and I remembered the night before. And even as I sang along, I thought, *Wow, the crowd was so much better last night*. But then I realized it was mostly the same people here, again. It was just my mind that was different. I was in a different place. I felt the gin hitting my head, so I leaned up against the post behind me.

"You're fucking drunk," the kid who yelled at me before said. I told him to fuck off. I told him he didn't understand what the fuck he was talking about, and to mind his own goddamn business. To watch the goddamn concert instead of judging the people.

I don't regret this, but I probably could have phrased it better. I am lucky I didn't get my teeth knocked out, though. To his credit, I guess I couldn't see myself. It's possible I looked like a wreck—very possible. One guy put his arm around me and told me that guy was a jackass, but I told him it wasn't necessary, and shrugged his arm off. I wanted to be alone again. I wanted to feel lonely. I sang along, louder this time. Probably slurred. I couldn't tell if it was the alcohol or my regressing mentality.

During intermission. I wanted to be sure I didn't say anything else to that kid, so I went back to the bar again. More alcohol. I asked for a PBR, and the bartender, this time a guy, told me there was a minimum charge, so I ordered one for the person next to me. He tried to start conversation with me, but again, I felt the negative taking over. I told him my name, then excused myself as All Them Witches was setting up.

I didn't want these negative thoughts to take over again, but it was involuntary, like a tsunami wave I could see from a long distance. No matter how fast I ran, I knew the negative would take over soon enough. I didn't want it to happen mid-conversation. I walked toward the front, near the speakers.

Where it's acceptable to be alone simply because conversation is nearly impossible.

Except this time, I couldn't get close to the stage. I got as close as I could, but stood back. I didn't want to get into another altercation. At this point, I knew I was too volatile to deal with that again. I didn't trust myself.

I remembered once when Jake and I had been in a bar, near the end. The summer before he did it. The DJ was pretending to mix a record, but it was obvious that the music was playing from his iPod. I told him not to worry about it, but Jake felt the need to confront the man who was pretending that the music was coming from his empty record player.

I tried to take my own advice, the advice I gave him. "It doesn't matter. Don't worry about it," I told him. "If it doesn't affect you, if it's not actively hurting you, if it's not hurting anyone else, it's not your problem," I had told him. I told myself these things now. But now, I felt like everything was hurting me. That every slight was a major assault.

Like I mentioned before, after eight years of knowing someone, personality traits combine. The good and the bad. I tried to suppress it.

I should cut myself off, I thought as I sipped on my beer. I talked with someone as All Them Witches set up. "Have you seen them before?" he said.

"Yeah, a couple of places. They always put on a good show. I'm from Milwaukee."

"Shit, why'd you come here?"

"A great way to see the country. New city, new experiences." St. Louis came back to my mind. A kick from the past.

The conversation fizzled from there. I was fine with it. My manic need to connect still existed, but I had given up on all hopes of connecting

with anyone. I'm sure there were nice people there, but I wasn't in that frame of mind. As much as I wanted to—much like I couldn't plan anything ahead of time anymore—I couldn't plan on whether I could connect with people or not, no matter how badly I wanted to. The mask was off, so I'm fairly sure it was obvious now.

All Them Witches started playing again. This time, they were playing their older songs, ones they hadn't played before on this tour. I sang along to the ones I knew, then swayed to the ones I didn't. I made small talk with a girl next to me about how they were playing "all of their old stuff—how awesome," which I agreed was cool, but she was much more excited about it than I was. I was too distracted.

I don't belong here, I thought again. *I should go home, back to Milwaukee. I shouldn't be here.*

But I stopped myself. *But I'm here now*, I thought. *I'm here. Stay present. Stay here.* I willed my mind to push through it. I couldn't. More alcohol. This time, I got a whiskey-ginger. *I'm here now, so might as well make the most of it.*

I knew I had to learn to deal with those times where my mind suddenly turned sour. This wasn't getting better. If anything, it was getting worse. It was difficult for me to admit that I couldn't handle it on my own. Even through my roughest times in my past, I've always been able to pull myself through. I had never encountered something I couldn't get through myself. For me, it was about pride.

This was different.

And even though I prided myself on refusing medication, for some strange, distorted reason, I still was self-medicating. I equated it to refusing Vicodin after a terrible accident I was in involving 120 lbs. of metal crushing my left foot. This was different, though—this was mental pain. And the pain was morphing. It wasn't a simple body repair. It changed as my head continued to process. This wasn't mind over body, because when your mind is distorted, it can't heal itself.

My medication came in the form of traveling or alcohol, even though the two were becoming a bit too intertwined. A *contained bender*

would be the only way to describe it, and though it was contained, it was unnatural for me. Compared to others, I did have it relatively controlled on the outside—but in my mind, I was losing it. I could feel everything slipping. I was becoming immune to this Band-Aid medication. I needed a holistic heal, but I was too scared to make the jump toward it. I wasn't ready.

It wasn't about how much I was drinking. It wasn't like I was falling all over the sidewalk, and it wasn't like I was going home with people I didn't know or placing myself directly in danger. It was my mentality toward drinking, and my dependency on it—and it was no better than becoming dependent on any sort of medication.

When I had first gone to see All Them Witches in Madison, at the beginning of their tour, I filled a coffee mug with gin, and though I didn't drink any of it, it was a comfort to know it was there. At this point, I wasn't so sure if I could keep away from it, if I was put in that situation again. I sipped on my drink. I knew I didn't want that to happen, ever.

All Them Witches finished up their last song, then started to pack up. My drink was still half-full, so I stuck around. I talked with two guys, older, about how the band was just like Grateful Dead, even though I was talking out of my ass. I didn't know Grateful Dead, but All Them Witches had a Grateful Dead sticker on their equipment case, so it was a fair assumption.

"Oh yeah, definitely. For sure," I said confidently, as the two men I was talking with listed off songs I didn't know. "It's at least an influence of theirs," I said as I stared at the Grateful Dead sticker on their equipment. I finished my drink in one gulp, then walked back to the bar. This would be the third time that I opened a tab. "Whiskey-ginger, please."

Allan came up to me to say hello. I told him it was a great show. He told me he forgot to give away the ticket, and that he still had my money. I said it was cool, that it wasn't his responsibility, and that I shouldn't have burdened him in the first place. I felt my mask creeping on again as my mind got looser, and I found myself deviating. I found myself talking about my "mom-friends" from the night before, and

this time, I didn't kick myself. This time, my mind was too frantic to realize how crazy or distanced from reality I sounded. We talked about Uber cars, and he told me they were self-driving here. I wanted to say that this scared the shit out of me, but instead, I said "Oh, wow. Cool!"

We talked about the set, and he said it felt good to play older songs. I said, "I bet. It sounded great."

He interrupted me. "Why are you so nice?"

I remember saying something along the lines of, "That's the most depressing thing I've ever heard. Everyone should be nice."

He interrupted me again. "No, no. That's not what I mean. No. The ticket thing. Why are you doing this?"

And no matter how much I tried to fumble around an answer, it slipped out, easier than before. The barriers I had built had been broken down the night before.

"My boyfriend committed suicide last year, so I've been touring around and buying a ticket for someone random, in his memory." I paused and I tried to gather my thoughts as best as I could. "I don't know, it just feels right. I'm not sure if it's right, to be honest. But it feels right." And I wanted to keep going, but I stopped myself. Their van was leaving. They were traveling somewhere else that night, so he had to go.

Another connection. This time, I didn't want to lose it. I didn't want to lose touch. I didn't want to make the same mistake I made the night before. I asked for his number. He gave it to me, then told me to get home safe on his way to the van.

The bartender I had talked with the past two nights was locking up the venue, and she also told me to get home safe. She hung back for a moment, to be sure I actually had a ride coming.

Jesus, I must look like a shitshow, I thought to myself.

I was grateful that everyone was telling me to go home. Had they not, I guarantee I would have gone out and drank more. I would have tried to connect more, in a city I didn't know, trying to find that fix again. I am grateful for the people I met in this city—all of them.

When I got home, I felt the need to text Allan that I got home safe, and I wanted to be sure they were all safe, too. I sent him a picture of Petrina's dog, Bruno, for unsolicited levity. *They had signed a card for him, so they probably wanted to know how he was doing*, I justified. I passed out and woke up at 7:00 am with a massive hangover. I called a Lyft to the Greyhound station.

Chapter Five

I've been to New York City before, and for whatever reason, whenever I decide to go, it's always during some sort of crisis. It has always been my safe-haven, my escape. It's easy to get lost in. Unlike Milwaukee—a small town masquerading as a city—you will never see the same face twice unless you plan to. I liked that.

This time was no different. I was in crisis mode. This time, though, unlike many of my other trips that year, besides Cleveland, I would be staying with people I knew fairly well both nights. Two different people. One I knew through work, Nick, and one I knew through comedy, Brian. Because now I knew I needed to actually connect, this was good.

This time, unlike Cleveland, they were not family, and I fully acknowledged they could kick me out if I got too crazy, no matter how well I knew them. I knew that, and I processed that, but this time, unlike Madison, I did not ignore my gut thoughts. Unlike the people I stayed with in New Orleans, they both knew what had happened to me. I had talked with both of them, extensively, the year before—probably a little too much (after a bit too much alcohol). No matter

how much they knew, I acknowledged they owed me nothing. Unlike Pittsburgh, they knew me from before, and knew what I had been like before. A different person.

These connections would, again, be different, as they had been in every other city I stayed in. I wasn't sure how I would handle or process them.

This time, it festered in my mind. I planned which masks I would wear with different people. I was not worried that they would worry about me. Now, I just wanted them to think I was sane, which was difficult to do authentically if I didn't give myself the space to fix my head.

As I had found before, I could not plan my mind. I had given myself a deadline to feel better again. When I planned this trip, I told myself that, at this point, I would be on my planned road to recovery. I told myself once All Them Witches finished their tour, I should be better again. I gave myself one tour to heal, to recover, to move on. As a writer, I operated on deadlines. *If I don't set a deadline*, I told myself, *I would never do it*. I planned it, as I would a project or a short story.

As the deadline approached, I realized I was nowhere near ready. I realized then that I could not plan my recovery. I could not control my recovery—it was dynamic. Unregulated. Fluid. Especially without my mask, I was different each day. Each day was a new struggle and a new process. A new obstacle.

The Pittsburgh show was the last show I planned on attending. Now, I wasn't sure how I would cope without these adventures, without this planned comfort. Instead of a final chapter, as I had planned it to be—a clean, happy ending—I realized it was only the beginning of a new section of recovery. From here, again, I wasn't sure what to do or where to go, just as I had been in the beginning. It was a circle.

I boarded another Greyhound at 10:30 am. This time, in my earbuds, All Them Witches played. At this point, it was something beyond the music. They were a connection. To me, they were a representation of all of the connections I had made in the past months.

"Man, I've had a rough day," one kid said to the air as he walked down the aisle, toward my seat. I was the only one to engage.

I took out one of my headphones. Though I was in no place to give advice, I said, "I'm sorry to hear that," knowing fully what I was getting myself into. It was another escape. Another connection.

He sat down next to me. "You know what? Shit. I've had a rough life." He pushed his bag under the seat in front of him, then after he situated himself, he asked if it was okay if he sat there in afterthought. I said, "Sure."

Ho'boy, I thought. *Here we go again*. All plans on sleeping and zoning out into the window evaporated.

But again, my need to connect was greater than my need for comfort, or for sleep. I could have ended it right there, as I had on the way to Pittsburgh. I could have pretended to sleep, but I didn't. I knew I would be on this bus for eight hours. I didn't want my mind to deviate, especially in a place where I couldn't escape. I wanted to connect, though I still wasn't entirely sure how, in any situation.

"Okay, but why's that? What happened?"

In my head, I thought, *Jesus Christ, I am not in the right space for this*, but I had taught myself that these connections would make me feel better—that no matter who I met, I would learn something new and hear a new life story. At this point, I was addicted to life stories. It was a fix I had to get early in the day to repeal my own thoughts. To remind me there was a world outside of my head, outside of my problems. An escape from dealing with internal struggle.

He kicked his backpack further below his seat. "It's just you can never win, you know?"

"Okay, but what's the problem?" I said. He looked to be about 21, maybe 22 years old. I looked back to my own self at 21. I remembered the problems I encountered at that time. Each seemed like a catastrophe—even the most minute ones. Finding a hole in my sweater was like finding a nuclear bomb underneath my bed.

But when your own problems have been festering in your head for so long, unsolved, it's a nice break to deal with someone else's problems for a change. I welcomed it on its surface.

Even better, in my head, before I had listened to what he had to say, I had already decided they weren't real problems. I thought I would be able to solve them all in one bus ride. Another project. In retrospect, I realize that this is an incredibly bigoted thought to have when someone is pouring their heart out to you, but this is what I was thinking at the time. It's honest.

"I just need a second to process," he told me. "Okay, no problem."

I put my headphones in as he scrolled through his phone, muttering, "Fuck, shit, fuck, shit," under his breath, but loud enough for me to hear over my music. I looked over to him with one brow raised, and we made eye contact. He sighed.

I could tell he wanted me to ask him what was wrong again. I realized I was pandering. This is something I had always done in the past, and while I had told myself that I couldn't do this anymore, I didn't know what else to do. I felt the need to help him. Even though my mind wasn't there. Even though I was in no position to help.

"Are you sure you're okay? You seem upset."

"I just got out of prison, man. I just got out of prison, so I went on this trip to see my friends, and I spent all my money. I can't adjust to this new world. I just spent all my money."

And before I thought about it, I said, "How long were you in prison?" Again, he didn't look very old, but I've been wrong before.

Without skipping a beat, he said, "Two weeks."

"Okay, that's terrible, but you can recover from that. It sounds like a problem you might be building up in your head a little," I said. Throwaway advice. I tried to connect, but I knew I couldn't. I tried to force it. My head was tired. My will was weak.

"For weed, too. Just a little ganja. I was smoking in an alley. I wasn't hurting nobody. Pigs." He kicked his bag further underneath the seat in front of him in protest.

"You probably shouldn't have been smoking in public," I said.

A faceless voice behind me said, "Word, I hear that," but I ignored it.

Focus on the conversation, I thought. *Focus on the immediate.*

"Well, I sure as shit can't smoke in my parents' house. My stepdad is a total dick. He's a dick, man. I gotta smoke outside. No place to smoke ganja in New York City. It's not like where you're from." Then, I realized he never asked where I was from. *Was it that obvious?* I thought. *That I wasn't from here? Where does he think I'm from?*

Not important.

"I still feel like this is a problem you could have avoided. Unless you want to end up back in prison, you should probably at least learn from that," I said.

And in my head, I admitted I wasn't processing his problems. I was taking my life experience, which had never dealt with that, and saying what I would do in that situation with no background. I wasn't truly listening. I think he could read that. He became frantic, trying to prove that his problems were real problems. That I should care.

"And, like, my stepdad beats my mom. I need to get her out of there," he said.

Immediately, I felt assaulted. As someone who had held all of her problems in, had kept them to herself, I felt like he was trying to pass his problems off to me. I immediately assumed the worst—but this is exactly what I had been doing before, just from behind a mask. My phone was filled with messages I had frantically sent to people, unanswered, simply because there was no logical answer they could give. What I was saying was illogical. That was even worse.

But it's easier to judge when someone else is doing it. It's easier when you cannot see the humanity in it. When you can dismiss it as selfish and dumb.

"Where did that come from?" I asked him. "I'm sorry to hear that, but why did you just think of that?"

At this point, I was fixed on solving his problems, but I didn't process them before answering. I realized I was oversimplifying his problems. I wanted to ask him if he was from New Orleans, but even New Orleans couldn't hold a candle to how quickly he was laying his life out in front of me, in rapid succession. At least in New Orleans, their stories seemed controlled, or at least like they were in control of their story.

This was different. I stopped myself.

Someone laughed behind me and it was then that I realized everyone on the bus was listening—outside of our conversation, the rest of the bus was silent. I wanted to tell the laughing man to shut up, and that he should mind his own business, but at this point, we were making it everyone's business. Still, a new anger welled inside of me. Judgment, any unjustified judgment, even it if wasn't directed toward me—felt like an assault.

"I don't know, but does that matter? He beats her. That shit's FUCKED, man. It's FUCKED. That's my mom, man!"

"Yeah, that is pretty fucked," I said. "I guess I'm just not understanding the connection between that and what you were saying before, though. I'm sorry it's happening—that's awful, and you should try to get her out of there—but I guess I'm not understanding the connection."

My head pounded, and I could feel the alcohol seeping out of my pores. I realized I forgot deodorant. I had taken a shower, but it was a drunk, half-assed shower the night before. I'm pretty sure I forgot to wash my hair. It clung to my head.

Focus on focusing outward, I thought, but this time, I was just trying to ignore how badly I smelled in a packed Greyhound. Everyone would have to deal with my stink for the next eight hours. I moved past it.

"Everything's connected, man. Everything," he said, with an air of unnecessary depth.

I paused, and I processed it in my head against my own life experiences. "I mean, I guess, but usually you have to make those connections for people. Sometimes, the connections aren't obvious to the person you're

talking to," I said, mom-like. I realized I usually didn't take my own advice on this one. I made a mental note to keep this in mind for the future.

"Sometimes, the connections aren't obvious. Man, that's deep," he said, cherry-picking.

I could feel myself getting more anxious. *More problems I can't solve*, I thought. Even though they weren't mine to own, I owned them as if they were.

"Okay, well, to be honest, I'm not feeling 100% right now. I think I'm going to take a nap. You can wake me up if you need anything, but I'm going to try to rest up a bit," I told him as I was putting my headphones in. He wasn't listening. He was on his phone.

I closed my eyes. In my earbuds, "Am I going up? Am I going down? Am I going nowhere?"

And I must have fallen asleep pretty quickly because I felt a tap on my shoulder two songs later, waking me from a sudden, heavy sleep.

"What do you do for a living? Where do you work?" he asked me. This is not what I wanted to be woken up for, but there was connection. *I need these connections*, I told myself. Though I wasn't sure this was entirely true anymore, it had made me feel good in the past, so I clung to it. But I wasn't really connecting. I was projecting, just as I had before. I was taking something I encountered in a completely different situation and applied it. It didn't fit here.

"Email marketing. I work remotely." He sighed, heavily.

"See, I wish I could do that shit. That shit sounds so easy. Just sending emails. I work at a shoe store. I sell shoes. I wish I got lucky like you did," he said.

"It's actually a bit more difficult than that. We send class action litigations, so there are a lot of intricacies—"

"Yeah, but you probably don't have to deal with the shit I have to deal with." He sighed again, texted something on his phone, then put it away. "The customers. My boss. Everything. You don't have to deal with that."

"Actually, I'm the main customer contact," I told him. "I deal with litigation firms and marketing departments on a regular basis. I have a boss, too. Every job has its ups and downs." I passed my tongue across the front of my teeth—fuzzy. *Shit, I forgot to brush my teeth*, I thought. I put in a stick of gum.

I felt my tone. It was unnecessarily authoritarian. I sounded like an all-knowing problem solver, though my life was entirely fucked at this point. While I was recovering, I was still manic. I was still confused. I was still running. It felt good to put on an omniscient mask, but like the mask I wore in Cleveland, it hung awkwardly. It didn't fit right.

"Listen, I'm really, really fucking tired so I'm going to try to—"

"Listen to this. My boss said he's writing me up for not showing up yesterday. It's not like I planned on getting stuck taking a Greyhound. If they wanted me to afford a flight home, they should pay me more," he said.

"Did you call them and tell them you wouldn't be able to make it?" "They *knew* I was on this trip, man. They knew I was traveling."

"I really don't have any advice I can give you, other than you're lucky you still have your job and that you probably should give them a heads up next time."

Someone said, "Damn!" from behind me. I ignored it. At this point, I just wanted everyone to shut up. *This wasn't the connection I was looking for*, I thought.

I put in my headphones. But in the real world, you can't plan your connections. In the real world, people are people. There are some you'll connect with and some you won't. *Make the most of it*, I thought.

As someone who has been a people-pleaser for most of her life, I tailored each conversation to make sure the other person would feel

comfortable, feel safe, feel accepted. A lost connection felt like a failure instead of a natural occurrence. But I learned something on this trip, even if it wasn't in that exact moment—you can't connect with everyone without losing yourself completely. At this point, I was all that I had. I didn't want to lose myself. I guarded myself.

I could feel myself growing more callous. In my head, my problems were the biggest problems anyone had ever faced, but that wasn't reality. In reality, problems aren't more or less severe. They're just different. No problem is greater or lesser than another. It all depends on the person.

There is a difference between making someone else's problems your own and helping someone while still keeping your integrity. The former was counterproductive. The latter was productive.

I didn't process that at the time.

But, if anything, I had seven more hours left—and I could only listen to All Them Witches for so long, no matter how much I liked their music.

I took my headphones out.

And even though he was scrolling through his phone, I could tell he was thinking.

"Hey, I'm sorry I was so harsh. I didn't mean it. I've just had a long week. I didn't mean anything by it."

I wish I could say we had a groundbreaking conversation, but we didn't. The rest of the trip was helping him sort through his problem, talking about the Bronx, and talking about the chili dog he ate the day before, which didn't sit well with him, he told me.

I told him about Jake, and he talked about one of his ex-girlfriends. This time, my Jake story came out effortless. The cut that these words made on my heart as they came out of my mouth was dulled this time.

I remembered what a waitress had told me after Jake and I had a fight in a George Webb, after he left me with two full, steaming coffee cups. "Your problems are exactly that—your problems. Deal with them now or get stuck under them." And while this was callous, I tried to keep

this in mind. I could feel them creeping up again. I had to keep moving forward. I had to keep processing. I had to keep recovering.

If anything, at this point, I knew I could not get stuck again. If anything, my pride would not allow it.

***

We got to New York City around 7:00 pm. I lugged my suitcase out of the Greyhound station and found the nearest bathroom, where I sprayed my hair liberally with dry shampoo. I doused my face with water, then tried to clean it up with some powder.

"Long day, right?" the woman next to me said, applying her mascara. "I always feel like shit looking like shit in this city. I swear to God everyone's a model here."

"Right," I said. "I'm hoping at this point, I just blend in." "I hear that!"

I walked toward the bar where I would be meeting Nick. We met at an Irish bar, where they all knew each other and hung out with each other regularly. I knew some of the other people there from past trips. Because Nick's birthday was close to mine, we planned on celebrating our birthdays, even though they had been a few weeks before. I brought him a bottle of whiskey. He brought me a ukulele.

As soon as I saw everyone, slurring, stumbling, I realized I had a lot of catching up to do. I knew this was the wrong approach. I knew I shouldn't rely on alcohol, but I told myself this was different than before. I was not escaping my problems, I told myself. I was joining in on festivities. I tried to shift my mind toward celebration.

Focus on the immediate. My head was regressing. Memories came back to me of times I had been in New York City, times I had called Jake on the side of the road telling him I was fine. Telling him I was okay. Even though, at the time, I probably wasn't. Even then.

This time, no one asked me if I was okay, and again, I was okay with that.

They had been drinking all day. I ordered a shot of whiskey, followed by a whiskey-ginger. I followed it quickly after with another whiskey-ginger. Gin and tonic. Whiskey-ginger. Shot of whiskey. Whiskey-ginger. Guinness, because I was in an Irish bar and that's what everyone else was doing. I realized I wasn't in control, but I justified it because nobody around me was in control, either.

I felt at home, but that could have been because I was too drunk to realize where I was. At this point, I wanted to be in control. I wanted to be in my actual home. I wanted my space. This was a temporary fix, again. A replacement for what I actually needed.

It was good to turn my mind off, even if it was because the alcohol was eroding my brain into submission. It felt good to not have to use my brain. To not worry about my surroundings.

And I remember we had a good time, but this was only in feeling. I don't remember too much from this night. I woke up the next day with another massive hangover. My mind and my body were tired. I took a shower, finally, but most of it was just standing under the hot water—appreciating the alone time, wasting a ton of water, then covering myself in as much soap as I could in the last minute.

Because Nick was in West New York, New Jersey, we got on a bus and traveled to Manhattan. We went out to lunch. It was a going-away party for someone who was retiring and moving to London. I didn't know anyone at the lunch personally, but they all seemed nice.

From there, I took the subway to Bed-Stuy, where I would be staying with Brian. *Thou must not grow roots*, I reminded myself. It was raining. Pouring.

Because he was incredibly busy, I planned on leaving his apartment during the day. I didn't need to plan where

I wanted to go. I knew where I wanted to go already. To a comic book shop in Greenwich Village, my favorite one—Carmine Comics, where I had purchased my first graphic novel two years before. To a sushi place in Manhattan. And I planned on finally visiting Bleecker Street Records, which I always seemed to miss when visiting.

But as I learned in Pittsburgh, I wasn't ready. Also, because of the massive amount of alcohol I had the day before, I ditched all of my plans again. I said it was because it was raining, but even if it had been sunny, I knew I would have come up with another excuse. I holed up. I retreated.

I told myself I had too much to work on. I sprawled my projects out in his apartment—the flyer I was drawing up for one of his comedy shows, the writing, the ukulele, everything. I looked at all of it, then slept for four hours. I woke up, manically messaged a few people I had met throughout the trip (more connections, but this time, distanced), then fell asleep again.

I should go home, I thought.

Compared to multiple other trips I had taken to New York City, in years past, this time, I didn't leave this place. In the city that never sleeps, I slept. I slept dreamlessly and deeply. The next morning I woke up to my alarm, then rushed to put some sort of makeup on. I was wearing the same outfit as the day before.

I met Brian at his work, got food, then we went to one of his comedy shows. Because I hadn't connected at all that day, I felt distanced. This time, the distance felt like a bubble, and words took a minute to process in my head before I understood them. I fumbled with the right thing to say instead of what I should actually say, instead of a natural response. We talked with the bouncer. I panicked when I couldn't figure out if the door was push or pull.

Focus outward, I thought from behind my bubble.

The hallway was short and slim, so I tried to hurry through to make sure I wasn't in anyone's way. I sat in the back as Brian did his set. We left when he was done. He said he had more shows to do, so I found another place to be. Again, work friends. We grabbed more drinks. I met Brian at another one of his shows later.

There was a comic from Los Angeles and I asked if he knew a few of my comic friends from L.A. He said he did, and he was judgmental. Like in Pittsburgh, I left. I knew I couldn't control myself. Abruptly, I

left the conversation, said I had to go to the bathroom, and, again, just stood somewhere else in the room to cool off.

"Don't fuck with my family," hung on the tip of my tongue, but this time, it was real. I suppressed it.

We got home. I slept again. This time, I dreamt, but it wasn't anything significant.

I should be better now, I thought. *I should be better.*

I missed my first Greyhound that morning, but luckily there was another one later that night, to Cleveland. I would be staying at my brother's place for one more night, working the next day, then leaving that night again for Indianapolis.

On the bus. Alone. I turned All Them Witches on in my headphones again, but instead of a comfort, I replayed all of the embarrassing memories from those concerts in my head. With a different mind, I saw what I had done in the past, and I couldn't connect with it. I couldn't connect with my own mind. Where I could distance myself from it before, I realized I could not escape from it, now.

Each version of myself was a different part of myself—the darkness, the parts I tried to repress. The parts I was most embarrassed of. An exaggeration. A caricature.

I should be better resonated in my head again. *Why aren't you better?!*

***

It was still storming, and as luck would have it, the bus broke down. The lights came on, and everyone who had been sleeping woke up.

"Hey, you got a ukulele? Why don't you play something for us?" the guy across the aisle said. I tried to convince him that I had no idea what I was doing, but for whatever reason, when you tell someone you don't know anything, they assume you know everything. Instead of dragging it out, I played the only song I learned—Spongebob Squarepants's

"The Fun Song." I played "F is for friends who do stuff together, U is for you and me..." on the verge of tears, stuttering my way through it.

We switched buses. In the period between switching buses, we were all drenched. I sat in my new seat and turned on my music. This time, Naxatras. Nobody spoke—everyone slept.

I got to Cleveland around 4:00 am. I worked at 8:00 am the next day.

Chapter Six

From Cleveland, I had planned on going to Indianapolis for a show—this time, for Pokey LaFarge and the South City Three. I worked the morning from my brother's house, then left at noon to Indianapolis. It was a five-hour drive.

And now, I just felt good knowing I would be able to drive myself. To be in control of where I would be going, of which route I would take. Also, it was great to be able to control when I could stop for food or for bathroom breaks.

As much as I knew I had to make connections, I knew at this point I needed to process my thoughts. I had to stay still for a while.

I should just go home, I thought, tired, exhausted. I could no longer manically trip around finding new connections. I had to build the ones I already had, again. The stable ones. The ones I could encounter every day, away from texting and messaging. I had to start from scratch, but this time, I had to move forward. I had to build something. I had to rebuild.

Just one more show, I told myself. *Just one more. Something different.*

Like the first All Them Witches show I went to in Madison, I didn't have any expectations, but I also didn't have that same manic energy. I was too tired for that.

Past this show, I now knew what I had to do. While I was on the road now, everything seemed clear. And it was interesting that Indianapolis looked so similar to Madison, down to some of the same restaurants. Madison was where I realized I had to start connecting in general, and now, Indianapolis was the city I realized I had to start truly building on the connections I had made. Not a full circle, but as if it was a spiral. It was at least a bit further than I had been before.

Pokey LaFarge was great, but my mind wasn't there. I wasn't focused. I knew what I needed to do, and this seemed like a distraction. I had a good time. I met a guy who knows Pokey, who told me he plays in St. Louis once a week when he's off tour for a swing dancing class. He told me that Kentucky Mae, Pokey's girlfriend, was in the swing class. I said that was cute.

We talked about seeing different bands in different cities, and how it's fun to see different venues. We talked about some of the venues in St. Louis and in Pittsburgh, and how crowds were different everywhere. We talked about which cities were our favorite to see concerts in.

And though I connected with him, unlike the past, I did not hold onto it. I took it as it was—a brief connection that I learned something from, but nothing past it. *Don't hold onto it for too long, because that's not the intent.* Though I didn't hold onto this connection, I still clung tight to the rest of the connections I had made on the rest of my trip. To me, these seemed different, though they were exactly the same. They should be cherished as a memory, a good memory—not as some sort of returning comfort.

From Indianapolis, I drove home to Milwaukee around 11:00 pm. I got back around 5:00 am. I worked the next day at 8:00 am, a Thursday.

***

I returned to normal life, knowing I had no more trips planned. From here, I knew that I had to keep going forward. I had to fix myself in a

stable place, around people I knew. If anything, I couldn't afford to take trips like that. I'm glad I realized this before I completely exhausted my bank account.

And for me, it was difficult to process that, while my "road to recovery" was officially over, I still wasn't feeling better. I still was in my head. Every day was a constant reminder to connect, but when I was working from home, it became a constant struggle. I embellished my trips. I turned them into a magical, mystical quest, even though I knew it wasn't.

And the worst part was that most of it wasn't about Jake. While I was still upset about what had happened, I realized there was so much more I didn't address. When you are with someone for so long—even if it's broken, no matter how many breaks you take—that person becomes so much a part of you. During this period, we didn't care for ourselves. We clung to the problems. We clung to the past without addressing the changes, even when we were apart. Even though I was telling myself I was living for myself, I wasn't. I was forcing myself to live for myself—for an exterior motive. To prove to everyone I was okay. I wasn't truly focusing on myself. I wasn't making sure I truly was okay. I didn't realize that at the time.

Now that I was back in Milwaukee, I was faced with reconnecting with those people I had neglected for the past half-year. Because I had grown accustomed to my maskless self, I felt bare, especially in front of those people I had hidden from for so long. No matter how much I tried, I couldn't put the mask on. None of these masks fit anymore, no matter how much I tried to force them. There could be no more facades.

I continued to travel—to go to different shows. When I felt I couldn't connect, I planned to see C.W. Stoneking in

Chicago, and while it was fun, it was another fix. I went to Boston for a work conference, but I only really remember that I went to see The Alabama Shakes. I spent the show making sure the kid next to me—around 10 years old, his first concert—was having a good time. I gave him a list of songs he should listen to, something I felt Jake would have done if he were in my shoes.

I went to various shows around the city where I knew I wouldn't know anyone, but again, it was another fix. I realized this now—now that I was home, it was a reminder that I have to build myself up again.

Why don't you feel better? Lingered in my head.

Focus outward, I thought. *Focus forward.*

August 13, 2017

Now, I was back in Milwaukee, fumbling toward recovery in a space that had once been ours, filled with places that housed memories and experiences we shared. Outside of these places, his memory still lingered in my mind, and the dreams I had of him became more vivid, more pronounced. I felt the need to write him more letters. Here is the letter I wrote for him on the anniversary of his death.

Hey Dear,

I had a dream with you in it again, but this time, you spoke. And it wasn't just a jumble of consonants like it normally is. It was your voice, each word carefully chosen and enunciated.

The dream was nothing significant. We were at the Pick 'n Save by my parents' house. We were sitting side-by-side in the parking lot—you in the driver's seat, me in the passenger's. We were in your old Buick, the tan '92, your grandma's old car. The one whose engine started on fire three months into our relationship, the only time you ever missed a day of work at Sendik's Fine Foods in Brookfield. I still remember when you called me—the only thing you were concerned about was missing work rather than your literally exploded car.

Shit, that Buick call was eight years ago already, but the root of your concern never left you. Sir Jacob Christ, charitable and kind, but only to those who deserved it.

In the dream, we were planning which movie we were going to rent and what food we were going to buy.

And I know it was a dream only because we never went to the Pick 'n Save by my parents' house and there were no Blockbusters anymore when you had your beard and there was no way you would have trusted me to pick out the snacks by myself.

But what was real—your eyes. Your face. Your laugh. Your voice. The way your eyebrows tilted up when you called me "B," but especially tilted when you called me "ladybug." The uncanny way you said, "That's not healthy!" when I suggested peanut butter fudge core ice cream. The way your whole face smiled, starting from your pure, blue eyes that squinted under your brow (which I'll never understand why you were self-conscious about that) to your smile accented by the cap in your front tooth from when it was shot out with a paintball when you were a kid, tinted one subtle shade closer to gray. And I even remember the way you smell—the Acqua di Giò cologne you got once every Christmas from your mom, your scent stained with the yellow Natural American Spirits you were trying to quit and cut with the gin you were trying to cut back on.

That aside, you were happy.

I could always tell you were happy by looking in your eyes—if they were unclouded. This time, they were purer than I've ever seen them. Focused outward, not inward. Connected.

And I've never been a religious person, not even spiritual, but I hope this dream means that somewhere out there, you've got it together again. That you figured it out. That your demons finally left you and let you be the Jake I know you were all along underneath the imbalance. Clear-headed. Happy. Somewhere.

And I've come to terms with you visiting in my dreams like that.

At first, it hurt. An aching, longing hurt that would linger like a terrible mosquito bite, an itch that would never be satiated until you finally scratched it open and it scabbed over and maybe a week later would kind of heal, but the scar would always be there. But now, one year later to the day after your death, it's comforting. Like seeing an old friend for a quick coffee before they leave for God knows where.

And I hope one day in one of these dreams, we'll meet in Webb's, and we'll talk over black coffee and early-riser sandwiches, sausage patty with the egg over-easy, of fucking course with an English muffin. I hope that, maybe, we'll catch a Red Fang concert sometime. You missed a good one in October. I hope maybe we'll finally get to visit Maine like we always talked about, even if it's only for a cup of coffee or a short walk on the rocky coast. Maybe we'll visit Bruges again. I promise not to fuck it up this time.

But most importantly, I hope in these dreams you continue to be as happy as you were—that you'll keep checking me when my dream self says something stupid, but most importantly, that you keep talking. That you keep smiling. That we keep smiling.

At first, I was scared I would forget your face and your voice, but now I know one year later, that's impossible. I should have known you would never really leave.

Even if it's only because you said you wouldn't.

Chapter Seven

I could feel myself regressing to my old self as soon as I stayed more than a month in Milwaukee. I tried to break it up. I visited my cousin in Peshtigo, Wisconsin, and I took a trip to Normal, Indiana. But I knew these trips were only a bandage. I realized what I was doing. I saw that I was still unable to cope with reality. I acknowledged I was still running. I didn't know how to fix it. While I could see the answer, it was behind a layer of impenetrable glass—something I could see, but no matter how much I tried to break the glass, couldn't reach it.

All Them Witches announced they would be playing in Iowa City in November after their tour in Europe, so I made plans in the city that day to justify visiting. I knew I should have been past this at this point, but this felt like a fateful extension to my deadline. *"You have more time to get better. Don't give up yet. It can still happen."*

I took the day off. I met a friend for lunch, and we talked about how I planned on writing this book.

"I'm really happy for you!" she said. "I think this will be a great way to hone all of that energy you still have. A good way to move forward." She had talked about publishing the book with me, but these plans fell

through, even though she's still incredibly supportive. If anything, she was a voice telling me I could do it. This was what I needed.

And I felt guilty saying I was writing a book at this point because while I told myself it was something I had to do, it was still not something I was actively doing. While I had a rough draft of what I wanted, I oscillated from thinking it was perfect to scrapping the entire thing daily. To me, this was the same as before. It felt like another bandage. Something I was doing for someone else, but not for me. Another chapter with an unhappy ending, or, even worse, no ending at all.

If anything, it was terrifying. I had spent most of my time at home regretting everything I had done in the previous months. Convincing myself I had embarrassed myself in countless cities. Convincing myself that if I knew what was best for me, I could never go to any of these cities ever again.

Focus forward.

Iowa City, All Them Witches. I got to the venue at 6:00 pm, and doors to the venue in the back of the bar opened at 8:00 pm. I ordered a beer because I told myself I could no longer do hard liquor. I wanted to be in control, at least somewhat. I ordered an IPA.

I felt myself falling into my old skin again. The need to connect was there again. I started talking with a group of people about other shows they had seen. Kadavar, Graveyard, Red Fang. We talked about the different cities we had seen them in. I told them I wasn't from Iowa City, I was from Milwaukee.

"Shit, why did you come here?" they said. I replayed flashbacks to every other time I told someone I was from Milwaukee, that I had traveled here for this show.

"A good way to see the country," I said again, as I had in the past.

I had bought another Jake ticket to this show, but this time, I had told people in the bar that I had done this. I hadn't told them why—until I did. Until I told them too much.

"He won't be here because he's dead. I loved him, and now he's dead. That's how that works." I paused. Silence. "So if anyone wants the ticket, just follow me in when doors open."

"Shit," the bartender said. Because what else do you say when someone tells you this? At this point, I was three IPAs in on a basically empty stomach. At this point, it was no different than hard liquor. I went to the bathroom and cried, again, but this time it was longer. This time, unlike

New Orleans, nobody came to check on me. The band was still doing a soundcheck, and they were loud. There was a door separating the bar and the hallway where the bathrooms were. I had my makeup in my purse, so I was luckily able to fix myself up before I went back to the bar.

"Are you okay?" someone asked me at the bar. "Your eyes are red." "I'm fine." I ordered another IPA.

Doors opened, and the guy who asked me if I was okay followed me. I gave him the Jake ticket. I avoided him for the rest of the show, outside of a few *cheers* I gave him when I saw him at the bar.

Focus on moving forward, I thought. Though I was doing the exact thing I had been doing before, I expected different results. The definition of insanity. It's difficult to move forward when you keep putting yourself in the exact same position, constantly pulling yourself back to the starting line.

I met a few people who were from Chicago—one was a welder, and one was studying marine life in hopes of working on a wildlife sanctuary in Hawaii. A brother and a sister. We got a pitcher of beer. We talked about the venue, we talked about the bands, we talked about the surface-level details of our lives. Then, someone else joined our conversation. He told us that he worked at Jimmy John's, but also that it wasn't his life passion. He wanted to be a pro-skater. I told him, very bluntly, that

I appreciated his gusto, then I ordered a pitcher for the table. More alcohol that none of us needed.

All Them Witches started playing. The girl who I had been talking with before broke her glass. At some point in the set, I got overly emotional

and left to cry again. I got back two songs later, with another fresh coat of makeup on. Probably a bit too heavy. It was war paint—slathered on in an attempt to hide any emotion that might seep through my natural face.

"Are you okay?" the Jimmy John's guy asked. "Your eyes are real red." "I'm fine." I deviated. "Great show, right?"

"Fucking great!" he said.

Focus on moving forward. On progression.

I had planned one last joke for All Them Witches. I planned on getting Robby to sign a note telling Petrina he was sorry for spelling her name wrong. Unlike before, this was not a deviation, but I had planned on it being an end to an era. A final chapter. Another planned ending that didn't work out quite right. I apologized too much. I felt guilty doing it again. Like so many of the things I did on this trip, I went with my gut. Right after I did it, it immediately didn't feel right. The masks didn't fit right. I now knew them, at least on a "I-know-your-face" basis. At this point, these games felt disingenuous. A fake connection, again. At this point, those were more painful than not connecting at all.

I knew I needed real connections to move forward. I needed stability. I gave Allan another notebook, another circle. He thanked me. I left. *Focus on moving forward.*

Unlike previous regressions, this is one I felt I could get myself out of. I had seen what it was like to be at home again. I had begun to build those connections again. I now knew I had to focus on building everything.

***

I decided to take the next day off. I was tired and, even after all of the traveling I had been doing, I still had the vacation to use. I decided to take advantage of it.

That night, All Them Witches was playing in Milwaukee, and, as I had in Madison, I would be going with Petrina. I bought two tickets—one for me, one for the memory of Jake.

The nice thing about this show is that it didn't feel anything like any of the other shows I had been to. It was packed—a new venue in the area. They only served beer, and the selection was limited.

I was sad the show wasn't as I had pictured it in my head, but I knew I had played this up as the final fateful show where everything would, for real, get better this time—the final go, my second chance of recovery—Pittsburgh round two. I knew in my gut that all this was illogical. I knew, if I continued this, it would be continuing to live in the past. I would never be able to move on outside of this. I would be the fan showing up at every show until she was 50, beer in hand, reliving every single moment from every single show.

I didn't want to be that person.

I realized that my recovery was outside of my deadline. I realized I had to take it from here.

Epilogue

Here, now. Milwaukee, Wisconsin. Four months later, give or take.

April, Friday the 13th. Even though we should be seeing spring by now, there's a snowstorm. In the background, Rush is playing—"Time Stand Still"—but I don't see any connection because now, I'm moving forward, or at least actively trying to. Mindfully moving forward, rather than repeating my mantra in my head. And while on these pages, time will always stand still because this is a representation of my mind right here and right now, I am able to review previous chapters and appreciate how far I've come, though it's only been a year and a half, give or take.

I have a scar healing on my left arm—Rush's *Snakes and Arrows* tour symbol, burned and cut into my shoulder. I had gotten it to symbolize my road trip. Jake had gotten a "Starman" tattoo on his left arm, from Rush's *2112*, a shoddy job done in some tent when he was setting up lights and sound at Sturgis two years before he died. I knew I couldn't get the same thing as him. If anything, his tattoo looked like shit, and I knew I didn't want to live with that, no matter how much I want to remember him.

For me, *Snakes and Arrows* was the album I often went to whenever I was driving. And to be honest, when I first started listening to it, I thought it was the album Neil wrote after his wife and daughter died, which triggered his cross-continent trip on motorcycle. Even after I found out that was wrong—that the album I was thinking of was *Vapor Trails*—I attached to it.

Now, like so many other things, its meaning shifted. A gut impulse that builds the longer it sticks in your mind, the more it becomes a part of you. The more it heals. I'm sure it will continue to shift the more it heals. It still has six months to go, and I'm sure it will continue to heal in my mind longer than the actual burn itself. I could tell you to look up Neil's explanation on the album title now (he wrote an article about it) but I'm sure once this book is published I will have already moved on to a new meaning for myself. I'm okay with that.

It would be a lie to say that I'm 100% back to normal now, but I'd like to think I'm getting better. I still work from home, so the thoughts do still

get overwhelming. Tears are still there. Nightmares are definitely still there. Flashbacks of finding him, in the most inopportune moments—you betcha. Repressions and facades—unfortunately, I still succumb to them.

Through art, through friends, through walks, and through a healthier and mindful diet, I'm able to move past them better than I had in the past. What once seemed insurmountable now seems not completely conquerable, but a bit more manageable. While I have not completely rebuilt my base, through constant work, I'm getting there. While I still am drinking more than I would like to, I am working on cutting that back, too. I think that's helped, immensely. Especially in Wisconsin, where we consider drinking a sport, that's difficult. But I'm working on it.

Now rather than moving forward, my goal is to move forward with intent. Instead of some unimaginable FORWARD, with no real goal, my sights are on positive changes, whether they are in my life or in others' lives. Many times, these two are interchangeable—the best therapy is to learn how to positively help someone else, to teach them what you know from your life experience and hope it helps. It doesn't always work. I still fall, too often, but I now keep this at the center of my mind. My focus.

The connections I was manically making throughout my trips—that root is still there. I make a point to control that as best I can, to control those manic impulses. To focus on mindful connections, even though they might not be the easiest to make. They take time, but they're more worth it. More sustainable. The important thing is to actually connect, honestly. Truthfully. Wholly. To share, to learn, to grow, to move forward through each connection you make, rather than becoming stuck in a moment or a thought or a facade. You must create your own home around you, with the people you trust and the experiences you build together.

In the past, I had felt as if I had to give everything to everyone, even if it hurt me. That everyone around me had to be happy in order for me to happy. Now I know the best thing you can give someone is

your story—honest, true, without shields. The only way to truly make others happy is if you are happy yourself. You must lead by example. The only way to truly be happy is to listen to yourself. To care for yourself. To improve yourself.

And now, I'm still planning on traveling but I hope to be traveling forward, and with drive. As I write this, I have two separate tabs open on how to outfit my car into an RV. Whether I'll do it or not, it's something that I want to do. A step forward. For me. Traveling toward where I want to travel. Expanding my mind, instead of retreating further into a memory.

I hope to continue traveling, to continue challenging myself, to continue meeting new people as I explore different cities. But this time, I hope to do so with a sense of purpose. With a steadier head. This is a daily struggle, but something I'm getting better at reading. At coping with. I'm getting better at communicating this to the people I care about most, which has helped me learn which connections are the ones worth keeping, and the ones worth building.

These connections—these sustainable connections—they keep me grounded. This grounding helps me move forward, with a solid base. With intent. I could not continue to wait for recovery to appear, for some illusive fateful show or event to appear. I had to take control of my own recovery.

While I still miss Jake like hell, and while I will never, ever forget him, I'm now moving forward.

***

This half was originally published under the title "This Road Must Go Somewhere (and other things I told myself)" in 2018. That text donated all proceeds to the National Alliance of Mental Health, specifically the chapters in the cities listed in this book. While I would never take back that experience, and while I loved the people I met and the NAMI chapters I visited through this experience, I found that I was not able to financially continue touring while also donating all proceeds, even if I kept my day job. To note, many of these chapters mentioned this might happen, most notably NAMI

NYC Metro. But, like most things in life, I usually have to learn the hard way for something to stick.

That said, please reach out to your local NAMI chapter and, if you are able, please consider donating to them. While donating to NAMI National funds important research that guides essential NAMI programs, each NAMI chapter funds their own projects and their own operations. Donating to individual chapters ensures these programs can exist in your community.

Moving Forward

Our better natures seek elevation A refuge for the coming night

No one gets to their heaven without a fight

-Rush, "Armor and Sword"

Disclaimer, revised

I'm going to fill this disclaimer out a bit more than with my first book. As before, this book is not intended to be a guide. As I stated before, this book also is not intended to be an answer to all of your problems. That is still something you have to figure out on your own. I stand by this, because I am only speaking from my own unique human experience, and for what has worked for me. This shouldn't be scary—this should be empowering. You are in control of your own world, and you have the power to make it as great as you want it to be. I still hope you are able to get something from what I've learned, and what I'm still working through.

I also want to mention that, as with any book, this is how I'm feeling now. It's very possible I will look at this book in 10 years and argue with myself. Already, reading through my first book, there are things that I don't agree with (and I'm the author). I'm okay with this.

My goal with this book is to capture where I am at in my own mental journey, right now, in 2018. I hope that this resonates with you, and I hope you are able to gain something from what I've learned in the past year.

Foreword

Well, here I am. Again.

As I'm writing this on November 4, 2018, I've just gotten back to Milwaukee—from visiting New Orleans to speak with their National Alliance on Mental Illness (NAMI) chapter and do a few signings there. The month before, I was in New York City to speak with their NAMI chapter, and I did a signing there as well. So far, so good.

For my first book's tour, I've decided to return to the 10 cities I mentioned in the book, and give back to their local NAMI chapters. It's not the most lucrative tour for me, by any means, but it feels right, and I'm lucky I still have my remote job so I can support myself on the road. It's not easy—but I'm learning how to sustainably balance the two as I continue to travel.

I'm traveling toward *where* I want to go, following a journey of personal growth rather than retreating further into my past memories. Part of this means taking time in each city I visit, and part means traveling with intent and purpose. This is a daily struggle, still, but I can feel myself growing stronger with each city and with each experience. I feel myself growing more stable, more secure, more focused on where I'd like to be—an unencumbered future.

This personal progression was my goal at the end of my first book, so I'm proud of this. I don't mean to get too sappy, but I've never felt more motivated or driven in my life, which to me, is much better than being simply "happy," as was my goal before. I not only feel better, but I see a world beyond my hardships, and I'm growing my world further than I ever could have imagined. I truly believe this is because I learned to share my story, to open up to others, and to truly listen to others' stories—to gain perspective with each person I met, and to ultimately transcend those dark times in my past.

I did see All Them Witches and Handsome Jack while I was in New Orleans, and I did still give one ticket away. That's more because, well, they both just released great albums this year (2018), and I've decided

that this ticket thing is a really fun thing to do. It's something I'd like to continue doing when I have the money for it. I like to give someone else that experience, and I like knowing that the person has no idea where the ticket came from. I love this—a faceless good deed that I hope the person will perpetuate past the show. I'm a sucker for it.

While I did have a beer while I was there, I drank water outside of that, which (as you may know from the first book) would have been incredibly difficult for me to do a year ago. Moderation was not my forte, to say the least, but I'm getting better at this. I think this might be because my pain is no longer a cinder block lodged in the center of my mind. Because I'm calmer mentally, I'm less focused on flushing this block from my thoughts—now, they flow in sync with my actions, at least mostly. At least much better than before.

While these might not seem like massive steps, for me, I'm proud of where I am now. And while there is still room for growth (as I believe there always is, no matter where you are in life), where I am is sustainable. And I'm grateful for that. I'm grateful I could move on from where I was in even the final pages of my first book, and I'm grateful that now I'm heading in a much more positive direction.

If I'm doing so much better, then why am I doing this? Well, after re-reading my first book (call me narcissistic; I'll take it), I realized I've traveled so much further in my mental health journey, far past the final pages of my first book. I've decided to continue past the physical journey, to shed light upon the mental journey I went on after my physical one was complete.

As I mentioned in my first book—the body can heal itself, but the mind cannot, not unless you actively focus on positive improvement. While for me, I currently do not need therapy or medication, I have not put it off the table completely. If you are in a similar situation, I want you to understand that I'm not against those things at all, and I acknowledge that if I do need them in the future, they'll be welcomed with open arms (and hopefully my insurance will welcome it, too. If not, I'm glad to know that NAMI provides so many great, free group sessions in the meantime). Mental health is more important than any sort of rules I've constructed in my head, and that's at the top of my

list of takeaways from last year. I've learned that this journey is fluid, is constant, is without expiration—and I've grown to accept that.

I've come to realize that this journey is dynamic. I still have flashbacks, I still have bad days, and I still have regressions. But for now, I'm able to move past them and lead a relatively normal and fulfilling life. It's still not perfect, but I'm grateful for where I am now.

In this book, I hope to welcome you into the world of my greater mental journey, beyond my physical "manic quest for reason," as I like to call it. I'll share with you what I've done to keep myself on track, what I still struggle with, and where I hope to be in years to come. I've also included some other essays that have been important to my own personal growth—past the struggles I mentioned in my first book.

This book can either be read from front to back, or you can skip to certain sections, as they are stand-alone essays. You can also read from back to front, or only odd pages, or only read pages with your favorite words on them (but I wouldn't recommend it). Above all, however you choose to read this, I hope you are able to take something from this, and I hope reading this helps you as much as writing it helped me.

Cheers, Becky

(Sustainably) Moving Forward

In my first book, I wouldn't exactly call myself a shining beacon of optimism. While re-reading even two months after *This Road Must Go Somewhere* was published, there were often times where I cringed to myself, either internally saying *wow, that's rough* or *wow, way to be a bitch, Becky*. (I admit this is a bit harsh, but we are all our own toughest critics.) As I'm slowly getting back to optimism, I look back on these times, squinting to make out what I was thinking while walking through these shadows. It's difficult to re-read through these times in my past and confidently say I'd react the same way as the person I've grown into now. I'm grateful for that.

Though often agonizing to read, I stand by those times and what I wrote, even if it was sometimes painfully raw and visceral. It's honest and real to what I was feeling at that time.

It still surprises me what I went through—it still seems surreal to me, even now. It would be disconcerting if I bounced back gracefully. I think I would be more worried if I hadn't stumbled, if I hadn't challenged these thoughts in my head, if I hadn't spent time clawing at the walls from the bottom of a well before I finally asked for a ladder. And if I hadn't fallen off that ladder a few times, refused it again, told whoever threw it down to fuck off, then spent more time clawing the walls before sheepishly asking someone to throw down a ladder? I don't know where I'd be.

But was I preemptive in saying *this is the end of my journey*? Absolutely. At the end of my first book, it was only the beginning of my sustainable mental journey toward recovery. Even as I start this book, I know I still have a long way to go. This isn't a typical story where the protagonist encounters a problem, goes through a novel's worth of hardship, then defeats the problem at the end. As I learned in 2017, there is no magical ending. It continues to be a lot of hard, behind-the-scenes work to get to where I am today, and I'm grateful that I had the endurance to do it all and continue pushing forward and climbing upward, with the help of those around me.

I acknowledge that this will be something that I carry with me for the rest of my life. As I learned in my first book, however, this does not have to be an overwhelmingly heavy weight. That it is not a burden to carry on my own. Sure, the stoic mask looks cool, in theory, almost James Bond–esque, but the real, visceral, vulnerable face behind that mask is still there. This mask is so much more transparent than I originally thought, especially after talking with those I care about most, those who saw me endure these times and are still there for me. Like trying to cover up zits with a lightweight, eco-friendly, mineral-based foundation I recently purchased, you can still see the blemishes underneath.

As you may have gathered from my first book, I left off realizing that to build any sort of recovery, I would have to rebuild my base again—meaning I would have to learn how to reenter society, learn how to rebuild relationships, and learn how to sustainably keep on keepin' on. At the end of my first book, the foundation I stood upon was shaky. I was actively trying to move forward, but with every step I took, the ground was crumbling beneath my feet, and I would fall back to the starting line. And with every trip I took, I learned something, yes, but it was almost like I was in *Groundhog Day*, the 1990s Bill Murray movie where every day was the same but also different in that there was frustration—that nothing was changing, and with every day came a different reaction. All Them Witches concerts became my Punxsutawney, Pennsylvania. With each concert (while I adore them as people as well as for their music), I became more and more frustrated that nothing was changing, that I wasn't moving forward, no matter how hard I actively tried.

To be clear, this was my fault, not theirs. They're lovely.

While it was a constant, it wasn't a stable base because it wasn't sustainable. There was no maintainable way that I could go to an All Them Witches concert whenever I was feeling down. If anything, I hope they're not touring that much, because that sounds exhausting and I want them to be well. But also for me, I needed to stop running, and I needed to learn how to reenter the world as a productive human being. I think this goes with anything—had I not chosen All Them Witches concerts, I could have simply chosen to drink alone in my apartment. I was definitely on the path to do so, and I easily could have fallen in

that direction. This could have equally been my *Groundhog Day.* It could have been waking up and pouring a liberal shot of whiskey in my coffee, with my temples throbbing from the night before (or even worse, still dulled by alcohol).

This *sustainability* is where true recovery comes in. I could not continually attend All Them Witches concerts, just as I could not continually destroy my liver. While I felt better at the time, and while I would still argue that overall All Them Witches music has positively impacted my life, and that alcohol in moderation can be okay, it was my *expectations* for these things. I expected them to heal me, but only I could heal myself.

Past my own recovery, I needed to be a productive member of society again—for myself and for others. I couldn't wait for this to happen, because only I could make this a reality.

At first, I was productive for others. I acknowledged that they were worried about me, and I wanted to be sure they didn't have to anymore. But as I learned how to interact with society again, this shifted and leveled to a balanced "for them, and for me."

This was difficult.

For me, I've always struggled with giving too much to others while sacrificing my own well-being. I needed to relearn how to interact with people, how to rebuild relationships with those who I would encounter every day. I needed to learn how to own where I was, to trust others enough around me to open up to them, and to learn how to take advice again. I needed to be at a point where I would be able to give them advice, too, which meant clearing my head and processing the thoughts that had festered in my mind for far too long.

This give and take, for me, is how sustainability is built again. That's how I build trust—through this honest, maskless exchange of stories and hardships. Often times, I am able to learn more about myself when I give my honest advice to others, and I hope those around me experience the same when they give me advice. But this equal balance—of caring for myself while also caring for others—is important.

And do I have trust issues now? You betcha. But with each person I learn to trust, those issues are slowly dissipating. I first was concerned that those who loved me would judge me, or treat me differently, but I learned most of those I truly trust and cherish still accepted me for who I was, even then—and for who I am now. I learned that it felt so much better to be honest and open about how I felt.

Of course, they still give me shit for how I reacted after it all happened, but I'd expect nothing less. If they pretended like it was completely normal and didn't check me for the absolutely ridiculous things I did, I'm not sure I would trust their judgment.

There is a stark difference between those who judge silently and those who joke openly—the jokers openly want me to do better, and the judgers are not in it for my best interests. That's okay—I've learned that I am in control, for the most part, of those who I choose to allow in my social circle. This isn't selfish because I'm building my tribe, and I'm grateful for the badass one I've been able to gather. I'm grateful that they've accepted me, too, rather than questioning whether they'll end up leaving me high and dry—or even worse, before I'd run away without giving them a chance to prove me wrong.

Those who care about me most and those who are *sustainably* there for me will appreciate if I am open and honest versus pretending behind the stoic mask I puppeted before—they are helping me build that base. With those who judged me or treated me differently, often times, these relationships weren't ever sustainable, so I learned to politely weed those out. And as I learned in the first book, while I can't make everyone happy without losing myself completely—there's also no reason to be a jerk to anyone.

As someone who has been individualistic to a fault, this was an especially difficult lesson to learn, one I continue to learn as I grow as an adult. It seems strange to say, "To be an individual, you have to learn how to trust people." Again, think of it as your base. Even the most unique houses need some sort of foundation—your social circle is just that. It is not weak to rely on them as long as you continue to take care of yourself. This equilibrium between sharing and giving is where that foundation turns from plywood to concrete. I'm grateful I learned this now, and I'm grateful for the people who have taught me that this is okay. If you're constantly tearing yourself down, there is no way you can sustainably build anything. You can only start to build if you accept the tools you're given—you cannot rebuild on your own. These external philosophies, meshed with your own internal philosophies, build a sustainable base where you can actually continue to grow. I still have a long way to go, as I mentioned before. However, through this exchange of philosophies—be it from great friends, my family, or great books—I feel myself growing stronger and steadier. My platform is stable, and it is fertile.

"Hi, I'm Becky, and I Almost Became an Alcoholic"

One of the biggest reviews of my first book was, "Wow, you sure drank a lot." I think that came as a surprise to those who knew me best, as under normal circumstances, I was usually able to control it.

Alcohol was always something I've used as a placeholder drug. Whenever I was uncomfortable, I'd have a beer to ease my nerves. If I wasn't feeling sociable, I'd have a beer to loosen up. When my thoughts and my depression got to be too much, *drink*, I thought, just like playing a warped drinking game.

Every time you feel sad or bad, drink.

It wasn't the physical substance I was addicted to at that point—it was how it made me feel, and it blocked out those demons. But physical addiction could have easily been my next step—I was inches away. I knew I needed to stop before the physical grip became real, before my hands would shake uncontrollably if I couldn't have a whiskey-ginger or gin and tonic. This could have been anything—I could have latched onto another drug or simply another unhealthy habit to mask my already unhealthy mental state. I chose alcohol because, simply put, it's one of the most socially acceptable drugs to abuse, and it's easily accessible.

Reviewing my journals now, I can tell I recognized the problem, even subconsciously, because as best I could, I covered it up. It's difficult to retroactively analyze myself, but I think this is why I kept most of my drinking to my own home, and cities where I didn't know anyone, or designated "celebration" times. Though I didn't fully realize it at the time, I was not being easy on my body. I was taking the easy way out, the weak way out—and ultimately, I felt physically and emotionally exhausted from hiding from my feelings. I was ashamed.

Again, I was weak then. Because I had grown accustomed to this weakness, I grew used to being weak instead of challenging and trying

to solve my problems. This became homeostasis and routine, which makes it much more difficult to see a problem. This was probably due to being in a perpetual state of hung-over-ness and being caught in the moment—the alcohol freed my mind enough to open my thoughts, but because my thoughts weren't clear, I couldn't work through them. I was simply reliving the moments in my head as they had been, without the ability to think of solutions. I recognized it was a problem, but because I didn't take the time to fix it, this problem became my homeostasis. My unstable vice invaded my mental home, and it trashed it.

I'm not sure I would have recognized just how bad I was until I took the time to study it, to analyze it, to summarize it after living it. I didn't give myself time to process because I was eroding my brain into submission. I beat up my brain and dragged it with me wherever I went—half-functional, half-awake.

I often say the best therapy I could have done was to write my last book, which included diving deep into the volumes of diary entries I wrote during that year—much like looking at old pictures, realizing that the punk phase you went through in high school really was as embarrassing and awkward as your mother said it was. You can't truly see the full reality of these flaws until you examine them later, until you review the highlights instead of getting caught in the minutiae. While I was in it, I didn't realize how bad it was until I mapped it out on paper and summarized it.

After family members read my first book, I learned that alcoholism is something that runs strong in my family. I'm not about to outline who in my family suffered and still does suffer, but it's telling that I had no idea they were suffering until they told me, or until I had been told by other family members. Especially in Milwaukee, where beer is not only a pastime but also so heavily tied to our culture, it easily becomes a routine to those who live here. Everything *but* the bars shut down around 9:00 pm in Milwaukee, meaning that if you want to have a social life after work, the alcohol scene is difficult to avoid. The rhetoric in this city is that if you want to unwind, you have a beer. If you have a problem, you have a beer. I had to rewrite this rhetoric in my head—I had to learn to kill this *alcohol as medicine* mentality from its root. It is

not as cool as Dean Martin made it look—in reality, it's a crutch that, the more you lean on it, will only make you weaker.

Once I learned to combat the problems I was covering with alcohol, my attitude toward alcohol shifted too, and again, this is another thing that worked for me but may not work for you. For me, because I caught it early enough, I was able to cut it out completely for a month. This actually came from a brief conversation I had with Robby, the drummer from All Them Witches, where he told me in passing that he cut out alcohol for a month. I thought, "Well, if he can do that on the road, I can do that in my own life, too."

At first, it was isolating. I feared people would judge me if I was at a bar without a beer in hand. I feared that I wouldn't be accepted by those who I had gone out with before. I feared I would be labeled as boring—the proverbial *wet blanket*. I avoided the bars, thinking they were simply a place I didn't belong anymore.

But again, as I mentioned before, there is literally no other place open past 9:00 pm, and I work from home;

eventually, I had to combat this fear head on if I wanted to maintain a social life. A month seems short on paper, but in practice, it can seem like an eternity—especially when you don't get out much to begin with.

What I learned? Usually, nobody cared if I drank or not. And if someone did say something judgmental? It's incredibly easy to dismiss this unnecessary judgment. Also, water is great, and waking up hydrated is *way* better than waking up hungover. If I wake up after a traumatic dream, it's easier to move forward healthfully if my temples aren't throbbing from the night before (also, strangely, my traumatic dreams happen less often, but maybe that's because I'm actually working through my problems).

Once the month was done, I'm fortunate that I was able to casually drink once a week, in moderation, and only in social settings where I knew those around me. Now, I actually appreciate what I'm drinking, instead of downing the cheapest gin and tonics whatever bar has to offer.

Now, sometimes I even get a seltzer and lime, which is something I never in a million years saw myself doing. Once alcohol was no longer my necessary crutch, my attitude toward it shifted. Now, I'm fine with one beer, if any, and I'm sure my liver and my bank account are forever grateful. Once I learned how to walk without this crutch—once I learned how to combat these thoughts in my head—I was able to return to appreciating in moderation.

Past the social aspect, I also had to learn how to address alone times without a full glass of my precious boxed wine. I used to call it "my muse, on tap." Even after I stopped relying on alcohol socially, it had become an integral part of my writing process over the years. It helped me loosen the ideas from my head, and it gave me confidence to put them on the page. But now? I'm proud to say that I wrote this book 100% sober, which unfortunately, was not the case with my first book.

It's difficult to write sober, at least for me, because I had always followed the Hemingway trope to "write drunk, edit sober." As a writer, drinking is so heavily intertwined with the writing process, even if it's just following the patterns of other writers. I really did not choose the right creative path to cut back drinking with, but now that I've mostly cut it out while writing, I feel it's much easier to write without it—I feel like my thoughts flow much more smoothly and words come out easier. This is probably from three things: (1) learning how to address my thoughts, (2) learning how to open up with others without alcohol, and

(3) knowing that my brain works much better when I'm not dulling it.

As with everything, this will likely be a constant check I keep throughout my life, with the knowledge of my family's history as well as my own. I've learned to take a holistic approach to this simply because I caught it early enough to combat it on my own. Much like I mentioned in my foreword, however, I acknowledge that if it gets out of my control, I do need to seek professional help. I've learned that this isn't the weak solution—this is the proactive, strong, stable solution. To continue improving, I needed to learn how to combat it, and at least for now, I've accomplished that. My goals aren't simply to make it to the next day—my goal is to continue moving forward, to grow into the person I know I can be, and to do this, I needed to address my problems head on. I'm proud of this.

Holidays and Other Difficult Times

I'm writing this on the eve of Christmas Eve. Christmas Eve Eve. I was just at Walgreens doing some last-minute Christmas shopping. This is normal for me. I procrastinate. All of the empty moving boxes in my apartment can attest to this—I'm moving in two weeks.

And it's said that notoriously the holidays are the most difficult time after you've lost a loved one, but I didn't think this would be true for me, despite what everyone was telling me. However, like most things during the mourning process, this shifted. And even as I began to recognize this shift, I continued to try to convince myself that this time wasn't any more difficult. Even as I began to recognize this shift, I'd still say, "No, holidays aren't that difficult because Jake and I didn't do anything out of the ordinary for them. For us, it was just another time of the year."

And this was true in part—we didn't do anything particularly special. Even though last year I cried in the middle of *A Christmas Carol*, I still said, "Nope, not hard." I justified my tears because I imagined Scrooge was suffering from the same demons Jake had, and I hated to see people judge him in that play. I hated to see the crowd judge his character, too. I flashed back to how cynical Jake had been on his last Fourth of July, which used to be his favorite holiday, and I immediately latched to Scrooge's character as completely misunderstood.

But back to Christmas Eve Eve, back to tonight, at Walgreens. I planned this trip to be a quick in-and-out quest—I knew exactly what I needed to get. I had gotten my aunt a box of sampler tea for her birthday a month ago, and I planned to get her this M&M's mug I saw a week before, as well as a throw blanket that was on sale. A card, too, because she's a sucker for those.

When I got there, the entire store was filled with couples doing last-minute Christmas shopping, talking about what they should get their parents. As I was looking at a Snoopy card I was planning to give to

my aunt, I eavesdropped on a couple discussing how they'd address the inevitable "So when are you two getting married?" questions they'd get from both sides of their families. Their reasons were lame, in my opinion, though I can't remember any of them. I found myself wondering what Jake and I would have done. Our reasons, I told myself, would have been far superior, filled with surreal facts and outlandish excuses. I also can't remember any of the reasons I came up with, so it's possible they were equally as lame as the couple I was eavesdropping on.

I never realized how important holidays were for me and Jake until this moment. While we never addressed it, and while we really didn't get into the whole gift-giving thing, it's that communal bond of knowing the other is there. Even when we were cruel to each other, there is something magical about reciprocated love around the holidays. I'm not sure if this is instinctual or not to couple up during the cold months—from an evolutionary standpoint, I guess that would make sense, but I have no facts to back that up.

What happened at the store next is incredibly embarrassing, and while I tried to cover it up, I couldn't. I cried. I cried, hard. Gasps, sobs, heaves, all of it. Right into that Snoopy card (which, don't worry, I bought). Did people notice? Hell yeah, they did. It was hard *not* to notice the girl having a mental breakdown in the middle of the Hallmark aisle on Christmas Eve Eve. Am I still avoiding this Walgreens? Yes. Yes I am. Even though I'm pretty secure in myself, I'm avoiding it like the plague (though it's right around the corner from where I live). Until I'm sure those who were working there have forgotten, I will be sure to go to the much less convenient Walgreens five miles away, or even better, not shop at Walgreens anymore.

And yes, when Jake was alive, we didn't treat holidays as anything special. We were never the couple to get each other elaborate gifts, to snuggle up by the fire listening to only *Frank Sinatra's Greatest Hits* album, to sip cocoa while watching Hallmark movies, as we imagined less superior couples were doing. If we got the other a gift, it was usually somehow, in some way, for both of us—whether it was a book I'd promise to lend him later, or an album we'd listen to later. An investment. If we got cards, it was probably an otherwise blank page, folded in half, saying something akin to, "Yeah, I guess you're okay,"

and accompanied by a cartoon tied to some inside joke we'd be forced to explain if the wrong relative saw it. A game.

It was difficult to pinpoint what I missed because it wasn't a specific thing—it was a feeling. Amidst the chaos of holidays, these simple moments kept me warm. I've come to learn that when people say holidays are hard, it's because of that feeling, not because of the weight we held on holidays while he was alive. After a person is gone, what seemed mundane at the time leaves the largest hole in your chest because it's easy to feel you took it for granted, now that it's no longer there.

Many of the things I found stressful during the holidays I now miss, even if they were not exactly the most healthy at the time. After two years of dating, he either refused to go to my family's Christmas, or he made sure to make a quick departure. This wasn't because he hated my family, but because his family had so many traditions tied to the holidays that he hated to miss. He loved these traditions, and he didn't want to miss a minute. Because I saw the root of it, that these traditions were important to him, I didn't force it. Despite this, I remember the stress of trying to plan out both holidays with both families—to ensure I was spending enough time with my family and with his, knowing he would never be at mine. For so long, I assumed this was normal—unchanging. Being able to experience a holiday without this for the second time is strange because it begins to become routine. The third time is when it sets in that "this is your new norm," at least for now. Even though I hated this about the holidays—a stress that I acknowledged few had to deal with, but was too timid to address—I missed it, dearly. I even missed the stress. I felt nostalgic when I wasn't having a panic attack planning how to make sure my family didn't feel neglected while still going to his family's events.

(To be clear, this wasn't his fault, and it's something I hid from him. I should have addressed this, rather than holding it in and saying everything was okay.)

Those first and second times are still covered by raw emotions (like me crying at Scrooge last Christmas), and you're still dealing with those emotions on a more minute-by-minute basis. They happen more often when they're raw. And the third time, I'm finding, is no different

(like me crying into a Snoopy card). Now, three holidays later, those emotions remain. And it doesn't seem like they will be going away. They're still visceral and real, no matter how much time passes.

***

During end-of-the-year holidays, these emotions are condensed into a two-week period—where you usually don't have work, or work is much slower (at least in my industry). As time passes, families stop asking how you're doing and start asking if you're seeing anyone, and there is the communal rhetoric that, after a certain age, holidays are for couples or sassy aunts who like to remind you that "[they're] not single so long as they have a bottle of Merlot and a Magic Mike movie to watch later that night." This can feel great—a distraction from the pain inside your head—or it can feel incredibly isolating. The memories you hold from your past life linger, the traditions from before fester—and the happiest memories can turn your mood sour knowing they're no more.

As I mentioned, Jake's family was heavy on traditions during the holidays. First, there would be the white elephant gifts with his mom's side of the family, then once her side of the family would leave for the night, there would be the secret Santa we'd play with his immediate family, mostly his younger siblings. I'd go home to get ready for their Midnight Mass, and he and his brothers would pick me up in their dad's Cadillac to go to an old cathedral downtown. This was the same, every year.

My family has never been this heavy on tradition, possibly because we're much smaller. It was easy to dip out of my family's holiday because there was no agenda-no set plan. As stressful as it was to plan out his family's holiday without neglecting my own family, I missed this the first year I didn't have it, and even more the second and third years. For eight years, this was my life, and it was strange the first time it didn't happen—and even stranger the second and third times.

Now, I've found how important it is for me to make traditions—not to replace these memories, but to ensure I'm continuing to make the holidays joyful, to carry over what I've learned to love from this past life and make it my own. This joy is admittedly more constructed

and mindful, but as I work through this, I'm learning how to truly appreciate the holidays for what they will be for me going forward.

Two years ago, I started a tradition making a gingerbread house for when my mentally handicapped aunt comes into town for the holidays—an hour spent with just me and her, crafting not only the perfect, avant-garde gingerbread house design, but also the story behind it. Who would live there, what was special about it, who had owned it before, and so on. Again, my family is much smaller than Jake's was, but I'm growing to appreciate this—I'm spending more time picking out presents for each person, meditating on what I appreciate about each person, and thinking of what would be the best present to gift. I've grown to further appreciate my own family now that I'm spending the entire holiday with them—and as an adult, I'm able to truly foster that relationship instead of treating it as simply another task. I've grown to understand what holidays truly are about, especially in a family that isn't truly religious (we have no religious ties to Christmas, no church obligations—simply family time).

I cherish the times spent hanging out in our kitchen, helping my mom make an overly elaborate feast for six, quoting Monty Python and listening to music with my dad, and catching up with my brother and his wife (they live in Cleveland now, so I don't see them as often as I'd like).

Again, as I mentioned before, these nerves from my past life do not numb. They're always raw, and especially around the holidays. What has helped me is to repurpose these events in my life mindfully—to ensure I'm not isolating myself, to spend this time appreciating those who are still with me, and those who have stuck by me throughout everything, and to give them a gift to show them how much I care. The holidays are a wonderful time to do all this. It's still difficult, but spending this downtime during the coldest months to build relationships—not necessarily romantic, but also familial and friend—has helped me better understand what holidays are truly about.

However, no matter how busy I try to make my holidays, it's difficult to avoid the memories lingering from before. The last Christmas Jake and I had together I especially remember, though there wasn't anything special about it—we were both "on." I remember, even though he skipped my family's Christmas, there was something about the way he put his arm around me during their white elephant game, the warmth I felt, the deep connection I felt when I looked in his eyes when we silently plotted on how we'd get the record player that was making its way around the circle. His eyes were clear, connected, unclouded. I've grown to cherish this memory, and I'm happy that this is one of my last holiday memories with him—of him as I knew he was behind that mask.

At times, this makes it more difficult because of the inevitable "what could have been" if he had gotten the help he needed. But I'm learning, slowly but surely, that I can't continue to have these thoughts if I truly want to move forward. I have to learn to accept what happened, to stop retreating in my mind and exploring how I could have fixed what happened.

These traditions I've formed with my family began to build the base, and as I spend more holidays with this as my new "norm," I've learned how to repurpose this difficult time in my head. I'm learning it will always, on some level, be difficult. But by staying mindful, I am learning how to enjoy holidays, despite this hole. This hole is still gaping, open, but I'm mindful of filling it with meaningful experiences with my own family—stable connections and new memories.

Mindful Rituals

When you've lost everything, it's easy to cling to a self-crafted routine. Because you made it, and you control yourself, this is unchanging, stable. And it's easy to cling to this stability once you've experienced how unstable the world is around you. For me, I found this stability in things like reading every day, making healthy meals for myself, and going for walks—surface-level, positive daily rituals that have helped me grow physically and mentally stronger each day.

After I returned from my trips, I realized I needed to ensure that my base was solid. Was true. Was honest. To do this, I needed to evaluate where I was each day. I decided that, for me, the best way to reset my mind each morning was to go for a walk before work—so every morning at 6:00 am, I go for a walk. This took a while to finally become a routine because above everything, I love my sleep, but with time, I've adjusted, and I feel much better for it. Rain or shine. Sleet or snow. Whether I fall asleep at 2:00 am or 10:00 pm the night before, this is now how I start my day, every day.

While this might work for me, I acknowledge it might not work for everyone. For me, it's the meditative act. Every morning, I walk the same path but with different music. I walk on the rails of the railroad tracks that divide the parking lot from the park, and I try my best to not look at the ground while still keeping my balance. My goal? To look forward the entire time without looking down at my feet—while still looking forward, toward the sunrise. It's a strange thing I started over the summer, and I latched onto it. I like this. At first, I loved the symbolism of it, but now, it's almost a form of meditation. I'm regaining my balance much better than I had, even this summer.

For the most part, I see the same people every morning. We wave to each other, but other than that, we keep to ourselves. Once I get to the park, me and the same three old men wave to each other, without saying a word. We send a simple nod, wave, then walk our separate ways, on the same forked path—and to me, that is an absolutely beautiful thing to experience just as the sun rises, as the cold wind hits my face. I live for these mornings.

Whatever it is you do that works for you—if it's going for a run every morning, doing yoga, writing, having coffee while reading a book—do it. For me, getting my blood rushing first thing in the morning is what keeps me positive and centered. Especially because I work from home, this is a necessity for me. If you start on a positive note, before you dive into the mundane details of the day, you will view everything else in a different light. If you go into a terrible meeting after going on a spectacular walk, this dulls the hurt.

I'm not a doctor—this is what works for me, and it was through trial and error. I tried doing yoga in my apartment and I tried writing in my apartment, but it wasn't until I *left* my apartment every morning and breathed some fresh air right away—an escape from everything I know I need to do and a time to let my mind ease into the day—that I was able to refocus myself on what matters in life, on what makes me happy, and how I can get closer to reaching my goals every day.

Sometimes, this meditation just isn't possible. For example, this morning (which, at the time of writing this, is early January), the latch of my door was stuck in the latch hole, meaning that I was stuck in my apartment. I could not go on my morning walk. I tried to unscrew the handle and the door hinge and everything, but without a power screwdriver (which I really should get), there was no way the screws were budging. I literally could not leave my apartment, which is what I taught myself was the only way to escape my demons. Though this was only a minor setback, I felt I was retreating into my shell. This was the first time in two months I hadn't gone on a morning walk when I knew I was working at home for the rest of the day. Because this just happened, I'm going to try to bring you into the scene that was *this morning*, and I'm going to try to analyze it as best I can afterward.

For science? Here we go:

First, I woke up at 6:00 am. Immediately, to make sure I got out of bed on a good note, I turned on Al Green's "Like a

Ram," as I've been doing for the past two weeks. (I can't get enough of this song.)

I put on my fleece leggings; my favorite flared walking jeans over that; my new Handsome Jack shirt from a show I went to in St. Louis about a month ago (November 24); my Alice Cooper sweater; another plain grey sweater; my good, trusty, pilled-up seven-year-old pea coat; as well as my socks, scarf, hat, and shoes. (Wisconsin weather, *amirite*?)

And as I was about to open the door, I twisted the knob, but the door wouldn't open. I looked at the side view of the door, between the door and doorframe where the latch goes into the latch hole, and I saw that the latch was stuck again. (This had been happening on and off for the past five months, but usually, if I thrust my body against the door, I'm able to open it.) This time, there was no such luck (*my poor neighbors*). I tried to unscrew the door, but I couldn't get the screws to move. I called maintenance, but I know that time wise, they're less than efficient.

Rather than acting rationally, I panicked. I clung to the idea that this was the only way I could start my day on a sane note, though only moments before, I was in a great mood. Immediately, I not only felt trapped in my apartment, but also trapped in my head and in my thoughts, which were spiraling to a worst-case scenario. My hands clenched—the first sign of a panic attack.

And it wasn't even about my safety, of the obvious fire hazard I was facing. It was mostly about missing my walk that day—how I would feel mentally without this cold burst of air in the morning, without the sun or wind hitting my face right away, without stretching my legs before I sat down to work for the day. I feared the worst—and without even thinking of how I could avoid it, I feared the inevitability of regression, as if I had no control over it if I didn't get this walk in. Especially on a Monday, I feared how this would impact the rest of my week, which was carefully and intricately planned to get the

most out of every moment outside of work. In my head, I scrapped all plans this week, planning instead for a mental breakdown.

All because I couldn't go for a walk.

This is not sustainable.

While I do think starting the day with a walk is an incredibly healthy habit to get into, when it becomes an obsession, this is when it shifts to unhealthy—kind of like how eating disorders or exercise obsessions develop. When the mind shifts to obsession, a once-healthy focus becomes mentally unhealthy. This balance of mental and physical health is incredibly sensitive—if one begins to trump the other, there's a disparity, which can impact both sides.

For me, I've always had difficulty with this balance, so being mindful of this is incredibly important to me. When I was a kid, I used to be obsessed with thinking I was a chunky kid because at one point in elementary school, someone called me fat. (Looking back on pictures, I was actually pretty skinny, but that's beside the point. Kids suck sometimes, and they're mean to each other before they realize their words actually impact others.)

I clung to the idea that I needed to be skinny like I thought everyone else was, so I would stay up late at night doing sit-ups, squats, and push-ups. My parents had no idea of this because I would make sure they were asleep before going into the basement and turning on MTV as quietly as I could. If they came down, I would pretend like I couldn't sleep and that I was just watching music videos. I would show up to school exhausted, unable to concentrate, unable to connect—all because I was trying to fit what I thought I should be in my head.

Though I was just fine as I was, I didn't question my behavior. I thought this was how I would be a normal, functioning kid, one who wouldn't be bullied anymore. This led to a number of issues down the road with my personal expectations for how I looked, and how I executed my goals. I convinced myself that if I did not do these things every day, I would spiral into a deep, impenetrable pit of gluttony and sloth, and that would be the end of everything for me (spoiler: that's not at all

the case). That careful balance between physical and mental health was seriously skewed.

It went beyond what others thought of me. I got it in my head that "this is what I need to do." (I wish I had the foresight to have this same vigor toward something more productive, like learning Mandarin or studying philosophy.)

I realize this is more extreme than walking every morning, but I hope you can see the connection I'm going for—sometimes, rituals can do more harm than good, however healthy they may seem on the surface. I appeared physically healthy and I was eating all of the right foods, but my attitude toward getting there was mentally unhealthy. I'm happy that I was able to snap out of this, and to be honest, Jake was a huge part in challenging these demons head on, simply by challenging their root and questioning why I was doing these things in the first place. I will forever be grateful that he did that for me. But it's easy to forget these lessons as soon as trauma hits. When it does, routines can easily become your life, like my obsessive daily walking routine. Something to fill your head, to cover up those incessant festering thoughts. I could not continue as I was if I wanted to be a functioning member of society if I had such self-induced cinder blocks in my mind.

It's unrealistic to believe I can take a walk every morning without any sort of setback. Inevitably, there will be times where I will not be able to go for a walk, and I should be able to learn how to cope with those times in order to truly feel comfortable within society, as an individual. That's the ultimate goal.

As I mentioned at the beginning of this book, I offer what I've learned, and I present what I'm still working on. This is something I'm still working on, and I think it's something most people suffer with on some level. It's easy to settle into a routine because it's comfortable, and it's difficult to change that routine because any change has the potential to fail. It hasn't been tested. These failures seem to take front row when you're first starting a routine, but as long as they're positive, it's through habitually working at them that you grow past failure. It's difficult to remember that all of your routines were once something new, were once something that could have potentially failed (even something as simple

as brushing your teeth or washing your face at night). They became comfortable the more you worked at them. Once a routine grows stale, this process has to start over again (unless we're talking about brushing your teeth—please continue to do this, for all of our sakes). It's never comfortable when it starts, but through each new challenge, you grow stronger. The only way you can continue to grow is if you continue to challenge your routines.

This is one of my goals for this year—to learn to challenge my homeostasis. If anything, it gives the brain a break to explore different ideas rather than those I force through my head, trying to force a stale routine to stay relevant when it no longer is. We often forget to look at what we're doing, and we wonder if there's a more fruitful and fulfilling way to reach our own goals. We also forget to reanalyze our goals, to make sure they truly fit who we are and where we'd like to be—long term, rather than superficial short term.

These hyperfocuses detract from your experience in this world, your ability to explore the world around you, your full journey. Is the world terrifying? Looking at the daily newsfeed, it sure seems like it. But that doesn't mean you should retreat behind a careful set of rules for yourself just because you're too focused on controlling the minutiae.

Should you still be mindful and work toward self-improvement? Absolutely. Improving yourself should be your number-one priority, because ultimately, you should try to be the best version of yourself—no matter where you are in life. But there's no way you can be that best version if you're not mentally present. And you cannot be mentally present if you are constantly trying to construct your life with pieces that no longer fit. Your brain will forever remain scattered.

Especially after experiencing significant loss, it can be easy to cling to a routine. You are in control of your own routine. It is comfortable. It is constant. But if you get too attached to routine, you may not stop to think if it has overstayed its welcome, or if you could benefit from changing it. If anything, to be a dynamic human being, it's important to, at times, challenge yourself and change your routine, to make sure what you are doing is best for yourself while also exposing yourself to a potentially different way to live—even if it's just cutting out coffee in the morning, or maybe cleaning your kitchen in the morning and reading at night.

I was talking with someone recently who said you should never walk the same path twice in one week. While I think this view would be extreme to be applied everywhere, this idea has resonated with me on a more philosophical level. Instead of continuing to do the things you've always done, you should constantly question if what you consider constants are actually helping you in the long run. If maybe there would be a more efficient way to do what you are already doing. If maybe there would be something else you could add to enhance what you already think is a great routine. *Don't fix what isn't broken* is a great philosophy to a point, but that doesn't mean you should give up changing or challenging yourself completely. To progress, you have to work on it, even if it's the smallest things in your life.

Why I Will Never Say, "I'm Better Now!"

The short answer? Because I really do not want to lie to you. I'm not better—I'm different. It doesn't get easier—it gets different. And this shouldn't be scary, because once I figured this out and accepted it, I've been able to learn which healthy coping methods work best for me.

The long answer? Recently, I started taking only cold showers because, supposedly, it's better for your skin and your lymphatic system. (Also, I just moved, and my water heater is now less than efficient. It seemed to be the natural progression.) I was told by multiple people who have done the same that I will eventually grow to "love it." That I will find it to be "meditative." That my body will "adjust to and accept" this horrifically icy challenge.

Three weeks in, this is not the case. I still dread every cold shower. I do this every other morning, right after my walk, as some sort of sick joke to myself. It is not as refreshing, nor is it as relieving as they promised me. Especially this winter, where my home base of Milwaukee hit a record low of –50°F, it's God-awful. Of *course* I feel more awake because I am literally shocking my body, and all of the blood rushes to the surface of my skin.

Sigh.

Because my blind determination is sometimes my biggest flaw, I'm sticking with this because I told myself I would try it for two months, no matter what. You can choose to have sympathy for me or not. Either way, I'm still going to finish the remaining five weeks, and I will probably complain about it every time it comes up.

I will never say that I like cold showers. Never. I will never like cold showers. However, I've learned methods to get through them, and I'd like to think this made me stronger.

I've learned that I cannot shave my legs in the cold water without shaving cream, especially not with a safety razor (I never used shaving cream, telling everyone much too confidently that "it's just another

commercialist construct"), and I've learned that I do in fact need to wash out all of the shampoo from my hair, even if it is painful. Right now, my shower times last one Handsome Jack song—usually "Keep On," but it depends on what I'm feeling. Once it hits the breakdown at the end, I know my suffering is almost over, and I should probably wash all of the soap from my body.

This is a stark contrast from the half-album (usually something from Dr. John or The James Hunter Six) shower karaoke dance session it used to be, but I'm learning how to get through it.

These showers are not getting easier, but I'm learning how to navigate through them so I'm not getting pneumonia. Now, I know what I'm getting myself into, and I know how to get through it as best as I can.

Each time I get in that shower, I'm equally raw, equally numb, and my nerves react exactly as they did that first, fateful January day that I decided to take a cold shower.

I don't mean to diminish the PTSD pain I still suffer, but I hope you can see the parallel I'm trying to draw here.

As with my cold showers, when I wake up in a cold sweat, or when something triggers me in the day-to-day, I know it's going to be rough. There is no building of callouses in this situation. You cannot build callouses around all of your nerves. At least for me, it's always equally raw. While some nerves may dull with time, others will always be equally painful. Sometimes, the nerves that were once dulled will suddenly stab with pain when hit from a different direction.

Since my recent move, I've had to change my walking path. I'm no longer by the park I mentioned in a previous essay (the one with the railroad tracks), so I usually walk around my new neighborhood.

There is now a person who passes me on my walks each day who has Jake's smile. It's not exactly the same—he's older, his voice is different, and he's much friendlier than Jake would have ever been to a passerby (not that Jake wasn't friendly, but this man goes out of his way to say hi, whereas Jake was more of a nod-in-your-direction kinda guy).

What is the same is Jake's squinty-eyed smile, where the blue eyes scrunch under a strong brow. This was the thing that mattered—the smile was where the memories lay because, in my mind, all of the memories I wanted to remember of us together were of those where he was smiling his most authentic smile. *This* smile.

At first, it cut me—in this man's smile, I could hear Jake's voice laughing. I missed being with Jake. I missed his sense of humor. I missed everything. The shock of seeing it repeatedly on another face was enough to make me change walking paths.

Turns out that even though I changed paths, I still pass him, because I'm pretty sure he lives on the same block as me and we live in a grid. I couldn't hide from it, no matter how hard I tried. I had to learn how to cope. I had to learn to cope with him making small talk as we inevitably realized we were both walking every day—as we built an unspoken camaraderie based on similar habits. Even now, almost a month later, this nerve is raw whenever I see him smile. But I've learned how to cope with it in my head and to smile back and ask him about his day. This goes beyond the simple act of acknowledging this person. I had to learn to interact with *society* again—to attempt to change the context, day by day, walk by walk, instead of hiding from something I would inevitably encounter again.

This is good. It sounds cliché to say, but learning to deal with these ultimate low points has helped me better cope with the lows that everyday life throws at me. The context has been established—I know I can get through it now if I just address it head-on instead of ignoring it.

As I mentioned in my first book, I still have dreams of finding Jake, meshed with surreal, traumatic storylines usually tied to whatever book I'm reading. While they're slowly becoming less frequent, they're still there, and they're still equally painful. I know, now, that as soon as I wake up from this, I need to take care of it at that moment. I need to reflect on myself before I move forward with my day. This doesn't happen every day, and there's no way I can see it coming, unlike the walks where I see Jake's older doppelganger almost every time. It ambushes me, guerilla warfare–style in a place that used to be a safe

haven—my dreams. It's not going away, but I've had to learn to work through it in that moment. I've learned that I can't shut it out, not once—I have to work through it every time instead of burying it.

Again, I'm not saying this is easy. It's painful, every time. Burying it would save me the immediate pain I suffer, absolutely. I think that's natural—as humans, we want to avoid pain, mental or physical. But the difference between physical pain is that most of the time, the body can repair itself. Mental pain can only be repaired if you work at it, habitually, with intent and purpose.

And sometimes, it seems even more painful to address this head on, when it's fresh—but often, at least from my experiences, this will help you from enduring it for longer. Working through it is a painful, short stab; repressing it is a throbbing, festering wound. The stab will go away, but the throb—it will morph into something different, if you continue to ignore it. There can't be a day where you say, "Well, I'm going to push this one back, just for today." Even if it's just one time, it still festers. Your brain cannot fix itself—you have to actively work to fix it, every time.

For me, my mental pain is mostly centered around one specific context, which is the pain I suffer from missing my partner, Jake. But like most things in life, one carries into the others, into ones I would have never expected—like my neighbor's smile.

These guerrilla memories aren't always traumatic. When I see a bag of peach rings, I think of Jake because it was his favorite candy. When I hear Red Fang, I think of Jake because it was his favorite band. When someone does the "Goodbye Horses" dance from *Silence of the Lambs*, I think of how, through months of practice, Jake had perfected that dance much better than anyone really should ever do. Sometimes, these memories make me smile; other times, it takes me back and forces me to sit down and repair myself for a minute. Though they're positive memories, they're equally painful to rehash knowing he isn't here anymore, knowing they're limited to my memories. For example, a few months after Jake had killed himself, I had to leave a comedy open mic to cry in the bathroom because someone tried to do a poor rendition of the "Goodbye Horses" dance on stage, and I *knew* Jake could have done a much better job. When someone asks you why you're crying, *that "Goodbye Horses" dance* is a strange response when out of context.

I'm getting better at this. But does that mean it's getting easier? No. It's difficult every time, but I'm learning how to better cope with it all.

Sometimes, it will never be better, but the goal is homeostasis—staying above water. That is okay. As long as you are doing everything you can possibly do to be better in a healthful way, you are doing a great job, and you are stronger than those who ignore it and hope it disappears. This head-on combat does not get easier—it gets different with each day and each hurdle. This shouldn't be disheartening to you. This should empower you. The only way you know your strength is if you actively work toward improvement and challenge yourself, instead of shut things out. By repressing your pain, you're also repressing your strength. And though I do not know you nearly as well as you know yourself, I know that you can do it not because you're special—but because you're stronger and more capable than you think.

I Belong Here, and My Roots Are Growing

The year following Jake's death, it was difficult for me to find a space where I felt I truly belonged. My brain was scattered, nomadic. Whenever I felt out of place, instead of adjusting, I'd run, hide, or leave. I tried to rebuild, but I didn't give myself the time or the tools to do so. The base I stood on, one I spent most of my life constructing, was chipping away with each trip I took, then reconstructed with cheap plywood. With each regression I made in an attempt to force myself forward, my base grew weaker.

The strong, stable growth I needed was not something I could force. No matter how desperately I wanted it, I could not force myself into recovery. I tried to force what I thought recovery would look like, rather than what recovery actually was for me. It turns out that when you push yourself in the direction you *think* you should be going, rather than where you truly should be, it's hard to stand up straight (especially after a few drinks, as I mentioned in Chapter 2).

When you suppress yourself, be it by holing up or through constant erratic motion, you become your own world, and you become suffocated in that world. Your roots—they stop growing before they can truly be anchored and stable. Much like a maple tree trying to grow in the Sahara Desert, starved, you cannot grow past your own world if you do not nurture those roots.

I'm very fortunate that, despite my stubbornness, I learned this quick enough to put myself on the right path again. This was partly because of my last tour—it was a push in the right direction where I forced myself to analyze my story, discuss my story, share my story. I forced myself to root again, and my story helped me grow as I continued to share it. By sharing openly, by listening to people's insight on my own story and worldview, and listening to their stories and views, my base grew stronger—grew roots. The only way you can better understand someone's world, however dissimilar to yours, is if you interact with it honestly and openly. Not everyone will accept it, and while that's okay, you should always be kind and try to see their point of view, even if you don't agree with it. It's in this cordial dissent that we grow stronger, together. If anything, maybe it will help you gain a different perspective.

The bravest thing you can do is to allow yourself to be vulnerable, honest, and true. It's scary. There are so many people in the world who seem to have it all together, when in reality, nobody does. The perfectly cultivated lives we craft for Instagram and other social media platforms—they're only snapshots of an otherwise normal life. Even if you're Kylie Jenner, you still have to take out the trash once in a while (I'm guessing—I don't know her personally). I'm guilty of this, too, simply because it seems logical that nobody wants to see the average parts of your life. You post the exciting things because you're excited about them, too, and you want to share them with others. This is no different than those you are comparing yourself to.

Everyone struggles, even if it's in a way that is completely foreign to you. That unshakable base of wanting to connect with those around us is the same—even if someone's story differs from yours, we all connect in that we all have struggled, and we are all trying to navigate this complex world. These deep, meaningful connections often happen in the minutiae, the vulnerabilities—not because of the pictures you post from your trip to Belize.

My favorite bit of philosophy is from Michel de Montaigne, who said, "Kings and philosophers shit—and so do ladies." Even though we don't see it (hopefully, at least), everyone has this vulnerability in common. From Mahatma Gandhi to Martin Luther King Jr. to Neil Peart from Rush, my personal idol, those who preceded us shat and those who we hold on high pedestals now still shit. We all have this in common. If we all share one common ground, it is that we all shit.

It's not pretty, but it's authentic, it's honest, and it's probably the most vulnerable thing we all do every day.

(Or every other day. No judgment.)

I don't mean this negatively. I hope that this resonates in that I want us to accept our vulnerabilities—to own our weaknesses as strengths,

or at least as something that makes us truly human. By discussing these weaknesses, we process them as they grow outside of our minds. Instead of ignoring them and letting them fester, instead of hiding them behind façades of strength, to share our true selves with others is to become more comfortable in even our most vulnerable weaknesses. In this review, in this openness and honesty, we can find strength in even our weakest moments.

For as long as I can remember, I've struggled with telling my honest, true story. This was half of my battle with the last book—I couldn't write an embellished version of the truth. I'm proud to say that I think I accomplished sharing my honesty and truth with you, as best as I could.

To me, it always seemed much more appealing to tell a story much better than my own—to mechanize a version of myself that I thought would be much better accepted by those around me.

These deviations gave me so much more anxiety than I already had. Instead of comfortably sharing my own story, I would house it on a cubic zirconia platform and try to pass it off as diamond. When I realized it didn't fit, I would often panic, which came off as manic, which often came off as crazy and disconnected with the world around me because I would fabricate it. There was no way I could be a genuine human being this way. If we're going to go back to the Montaigne passage, you could say I was emotionally constipated.

I'm fortunate that, for the most part, I've grown out of this, and I have a great group of friends who check me when it comes back, though it's been coming back less and less as I get older, as I learn to accept my true self and be proud of my own life's story. It wasn't until I started being wholly honest that I realized my story is worth telling. And I realized that this story was much less stressful to maintain compared to the tangled web of messy stories I had fabricated.

Especially as a natural storyteller, I loved the idea of a good story, and because I didn't own my own story, I would simply adopt a new one. But as any good storyteller knows, a good story has to have a base. I did not have that. And the best story you can tell is a true story, one that is rooted in honesty, even in fiction. If the protagonist isn't rooted

in at least a little truth, if the character is constantly hiding his or her vulnerabilities, the reader cannot make a connection. And for yourself, if you're crafting your own story, you cannot challenge a crafted persona on any sort of higher level. Your character can only go so far.

What have I learned from this? I've learned that I think my actual, vulnerable self is pretty kickass. I'm stronger than I gave myself credit for, and I'm a lot smarter than I gave myself credit for.

I learned, through being open and honest, that the honest and true stories *are* the most interesting—they're filled with vulnerabilities and awkward moments, and they're *yours*. It's easy to think that you're boring because you live in your head every day. You live with yourself and your thoughts, and you know yourself better than anyone else ever will. But nobody else can hear those thoughts, or see your inner fears. By opening up about these honestly, this will (hopefully, sometimes) give them perspective. Even if it doesn't, in the end, it is much less stressful for you. You can leave that interaction with some sense of absolution—a "Well, that didn't work out" versus "Oh, that mask really didn't go over well. Which mask should I wear next?"

Even if your goal was to only cover up your weaknesses, by doing so, you also cover up strengths that you didn't even know you had.

Once I was able open up about who I truly am, I noticed that I'm much more creative, and it's so much easier to accomplish the things I actually want to accomplish. It's easier for me to create something that I'm 100% behind because I'm not trying to make it into something it's not—I put my honest, true voice behind it. Even if it isn't well received, I'm proud of it because I know it's *me*. And if it is received well? Even better, because that means people like me for me, rather than the false voice I was parroting. Because less of my energy is focused on building a persona, on hiding my vulnerabilities, I've found that I really love living in this world. I love living it as who I am today, and I look forward to continuing to explore who I am and continuing to challenge myself to be a stable, more honest, more true version of myself. I hope that this resonates with those I meet, and if it doesn't, I honestly know that maybe this person is someone I shouldn't force a relationship with.

However, back to Montaigne's statement, "Kings and philosophers shit—and so do ladies," even though we all take a deuce now and then, it's important to be mindful of those around you. You can't take a shit in the middle of the party and expect everyone to be totally cool with it. Metaphorically, this is no different than shouting your vulnerabilities to or at others, unsolicited. This is something I also had to learn the hard way—when I would go to a bar, order a gin and tonic, and say "this is for my dead boyfriend, Jake," there was no context established. There was no base for people to work off of, and if anything, you'd probably attract all of the wrong people if you continued to do this.

If you read my first book, I had a very raw chapter about my experience in Iowa City, near the end. I was just learning how to open up about what had happened to me, but I was struggling. I had broken down those walls, but because I was without a map, without navigation through the world outside my mind, I shouted out my problems to everyone—to strangers, to those whom I didn't know, not even their first names. In a manic panic, I exposed myself, and after I realized what I had done, I retreated back into my mind.

I am not saying you should completely filter yourself, but you should be mindful of those around you while still being authentic to yourself. It is not authentic to shout your problems at people without stopping to listen to what they have to say. One is manic, one is mindful. I think you know which is which—I'm sure I don't have to spell this out for you because you're probably much smarter than me.

Moving forward and sharing yourself is a give-and-take experience. There's a reason it's called *sharing*, not thrusting your problems onto someone else. There's a stark difference. Instead of stopping to listen to those around me, in the past, I simply kept going—I've found I'm less mindful about sharing when I don't care for myself, when my base is shaky because I'm not sleeping enough, when I'm working too hard, or when I'm not letting myself process my own internal thoughts before I let them out.

The purpose of exposing your vulnerabilities is to truly connect with someone, which is difficult if you do not give them an opportunity to share their own stories. This pitting of life stories—this is how you learn more about the world around you. This is how you expand your world. This is how you strengthen your own beliefs.

While I was in inpatient the week after I found Jake, there was a psychiatrist I was assigned to during this time, for one-on-one sessions. I was grateful for her in that she was one of the few who respected that I did not want to take medication, and she was incredibly insightful despite never experiencing something like what I had. What she said transcended individual events, and is something I try to keep in mind as I continue to move forward. I'm sure it's something all of you have heard at some point, but she told me that a stable life is a three-legged stool. Each leg has to be equally balanced for it to be stable. One leg is physical health and basic needs are met, one leg is a sense of purpose, and one leg is an emotional support system. If any of these fall by the wayside, the stool will tip over.

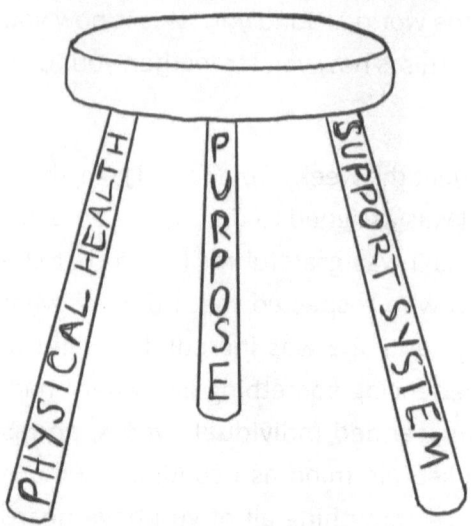

And this makes sense. As organic human beings, these three legs are our sustenance. A plant cannot grow its roots without sunlight, without water, without nourishment. No matter how much sunlight and nourishment a plant has, if it doesn't get water, it will die.

Through these three legs—physical health, purpose, and support system—these are your source of sustenance, what makes your roots grow deeper. This should not be suffocating, and this does not mean that you are set in your place forever. Your roots are simply attached

to your base, and your base can be mobile. The more your roots grow into that, the stronger your foundation will be. While I spent so much time fearing these roots, suppressing their growth, I was slipping on ice. These roots died as soon as they started to form, and this was by design. I was scared to root down to anything because

I had crafted in my mind that "this is how you get old quick." But that's not true. You get old quick by letting your problems consume you—and that doesn't age well.

While my roots are not fully formed, they're grounded. They're stable, and they're growing deeper. And that allows me to stand taller. Even when I am having my roughest days, they are not nearly as rough knowing I have solidity beneath me. The darkness is made much brighter when you have something to catch your fall—whether it is a support system, physical health, or a sense of purpose. And none of these need to be grandiose. They just have to be there, and you have to focus on growing them every day.

These do not appear magically—you have to build these yourself, and with great intention. I am happy to say that now, I feel like I do belong. And I can confidently say "thou must grow roots," but this is something that I continue to be mindful on. A constant check. My focus.

Music and Healing

If you read my first book, you'll know that music was truly what taught me how to enter society again. I'm not unique in this. Since the beginning of time, music has been a unifying force—when there aren't words to explain how we are feeling, music seems to fill the place and connect people from completely different walks of life. We can trace the history and migration patterns of our early ancestors through the different musical and artistic trends they left behind, from past to present.

Before writing this chapter, I meant to read a book on one example of how music is impacted by migration (*Chicago Blues: The City & Its Music*—it looks really great), but I never got around to it. Maybe this will be better—maybe then this will be 100% from my heart, instead of from a book I've been neglecting since I purchased it two years ago.

At its core, music binds us together. Chicago blues with Delta influences. New Orleans jazz with Creole influences. Eastern instruments integrating into psychedelic rock as those philosophies integrated with our society. Even if it's just a killer guitar riff or an amazing harmonica solo or even playing spoons and stomping to a beat around a campfire, these sounds unify us—they tug our hearts out of our chests and sew them carefully onto our sleeves.

It's a natural human thing—we want to connect, we want to be a community, and music is our unifying language. It is a powerful, portable force that, no matter where you are from, hits the complete emotional spectrum without speaking a word. That is the most beautiful thing about music—you don't have to say anything. When there's a song on that resonates, you know it, and it resonates with those who know it, too. That common ground is already established before either of you say a word. You just have to nod to the beat and thumbs-up the person next to you. *Bam*—you're friends for that moment. You learn something about that person by the way the person processes the song, by how you process the song.

I was raised in a musical household. For as long as I can remember, I've had a violin in my hand. My mother plays piano and my father plays guitar. One of my first memories is singing "Nowhere Man" as my father accompanied with his guitar, the music laid out in a huge Beatles anthology that I treated as my Bible growing up, even before I could fully read music and understand time and key signatures. I remember feeling the hardships of "Nowhere Man" far before my young world was able to connect with the protagonist's hardships, simply through the way the music made me feel.

In my memory of this moment, it doesn't feel like I had been singing it for the first time, so I'm assuming this is something that I asked for specifically, repeatedly, as a child. This was the first song I can remember actually connecting with—a song that taught me there was a world outside of my little six-year-old sheltered life. Looking back on it, I cannot help but think of how I felt within this memory.

A bit later, in grade school and middle school, I played violin with others at old folks' homes and funerals. Many of my first social lessons—they were through music. You do not play over someone; you play with someone. You follow the same beat, and you agree on a key. If someone openly criticizes you from the audience as you play, you keep playing and try to make it better while staying true to the song's integrity as best you can. You cannot stop and leave—you have to keep playing until the song is done (old folks' homes are brutal—to be clear, this never happened at any funeral I played at). This also taught me an important lesson that I didn't internalize until recently—as I've mentioned before, you cannot connect with everyone, even if you're speaking the universal language of music. But that unifier—it transcends culture or language or past experiences.

When I was in high school, I branched out to chamber and symphonic orchestra. The bond you have with your stand partner is usually tied to the music you play—your bows have to move in sync, you have to agree on who is best suited to flip the page, and, even on a minor level, you have to make sure you're spaced apart enough to not bump into your partner while still sitting close enough to look like a unit. The feeling you have when the entire orchestra nails a song is euphoric. The feeling you have when you notice your bow is the only one moving out of sync, or when your flat note resonates over the otherwise perfect harmony, is the ultimate low. Your individual instrument's voice is unique, and it adds to the dynamic, overall sound, for better or for worse.

If your orchestra is good, you don't care who gets the solo—you're proud for the person who achieved that, and you back that person up with as much energy as was put into the solo (or, if the person flubs it up, you play around the solo—you go with it, because everyone works harmoniously together).

Though it would be a lie to say I lived a hard life growing up (I lived a very fortunate life that I'm incredibly grateful for), music made those typical teenage-angst years much more bearable knowing that artists like Janis Joplin had encountered something similar to what I was feeling at that time, even if only in feeling, and they were able to make something out of it. It made it easier knowing I would be able to put these feelings into Vivaldi's "The Four Seasons"—and that I would be able to process it in every crescendo, every decrescendo, every rest, in a way that words just couldn't do.

My favorite music, the music that resonates with me the most, drove me to write my first book. While writing my first book, I thought, *Okay, now what do I do with this pain, and how can I make it resonate with others?* This teamwork I found through playing with others—this taught me how important it is to rely on others to create a truly dynamic piece, whether it's finding an awesome editor or an awesome friend who agrees to read that piece with honest feedback.

For me, I've always struggled with social anxiety, which may come as a surprise to some because I've covered this up with multiple masks, as I mentioned before. And though it seems like a contradiction, I'm actually naturally a social person, so this anxiety stabbed me every time I tried to do what I wanted to do—to talk with people, to connect with people.

What music taught me is that sometimes, the silences are the most powerful answers, the ones that hold the most weight. The thoughtful pause that is found in rests or in between songs. And what blues taught me is that sometimes, the best response you can give to someone is, "Man, that's rough. I'm sorry to hear that." That feeling the blues

gives—that shared pain—creates a base community, a place for your pain to sit and grow into something else (hopefully more beautiful than it once was, if you treat it right and you care for it).

On the other side of the spectrum, Monty Python's Eric Idle wrote the song, "Always Look On The Bright Side Of

Life," which was sung at the end of *Life of Brian*, where his character was trying to cheer up those who were being crucified around him as he was hanging from a cross himself. This, while not traditional blues, holds that same integrity, even though it's completely different. The beauty of it is that I can't explain why I feel that way, I just *know* it. You may not agree with me, but that's okay. The way I view the world is shaped by my relationship with music—it was essentially a third parent to me. It helped me grow into who I am today.

This is why during my trips in 2017, I ran after music. For Jake and me, music was also our language. We learned more about each other in the earliest days of dating by exchanging albums back and forth, by watching music documentaries, by going to concerts. For me, music had always been my home, and by sharing music with him, this meant I was letting him into my home. I believe he did the same with me. I remember how incredibly moved I was when he finally invited me to his family's annual Fourth of July celebration, which involved blasting music across the lake his family lived on, finished off by sitting around a fire listening only to Pink Floyd, with casual conversation flowing over the music as if in harmony. This is what he lived for, and I knew something was wrong when he said he didn't love it anymore.

We built common interests through the bands we learned about together and through the shows we went to, and these experiences led us to visit places we had never gone before, in venues we had never known existed. They built a shared philosophy on how we should interact in society, even if this philosophy was based on a Red Fang concert. You treat people with respect, you work with the group, you stand up for people when they are being mistreated. You saw all of this there.

Even in this small microcosm, this taught me much more than I realized at the time. This was similar to my experience with orchestra—it's difficult to put into words the bond you feel with those you play music

with, just as it's difficult to put into words the bond you feel when you share music with someone. You have to come together as individuals to truly make a dynamic experience—whether it's in the mosh pit or in playing Handel's *Messiah* in a concert hall.

Especially for him, past the times I went to concerts with him, his family worked in music production. I remember he once told me that he feared he would get bored of concerts as he worked longer in the industry. To my knowledge, this never happened, and I guess that can be the one silver lining out of all of this. Until his final breaths, he still loved the shit out of a great live show. I will not try to dissect why, because that's unfair, and he's not here to speak on that. I'm learning more and more that while I did know him, there were parts of him that I will never fully know, and I'm coming to terms with that.

But for me, music has always been my safe space. It's where I knew I wouldn't be expected to speak, but I knew I would still be able to feel the community around me. The spotlight—it wasn't on me. I could be a fly on the wall and still feel like I was a part of the experience, and that experience would be personal and pitted against my own ones. The person next to me—I can tell if they're feeling it, too. We wouldn't have to say it—we would just have to exchange eye contact, as our implied *hell yeah*.

During a time when I didn't know what was happening, music became my base, my motivation that I could make something out of this hurt—that I could move forward, that I could progress. During a time when I couldn't put my hurt into words, music did that for me. *Honest* music. I was lucky that the bands I followed were honest musicians, but again, this is a chicken or the egg thing (because I'm not sure I would have followed musicians who weren't honest).

Had I been in a slightly better place, I think I would have processed this better. I'm fortunate that I can process it a little better now. Right now, I'm grateful for Chico Hamilton's *Nomad* album, which is blasting through the speakers as I'm typing this. Even though the person sitting on my couch right now is calling it "elevator music," it makes me happy. And right now, despite the shade my couch companion is throwing at it, I'm grateful for every single note Chico is playing.

Loving After Losing

I do not have a ready answer to this, so I'm hoping that writing this chapter will help me find some sort of answer in my head, or at least the beginning of one. Right now, a little more than two years after Jake passed so suddenly, I still have difficulties truly loving those around me.

I do love my parents, but I acknowledge at one point they will part from this earth. I love my closest friends, but again, I know they, too, will depart eventually. It is not that I don't care about them. I do—deeply, intensely, and I'm incredibly grateful for them—but I acknowledge that there is an expiration date to every relationship, whether it's through a falling out or through more organic means. I try to keep this out of my mind, but even after about 2½ years, this pain is still fresh, and this thought still lingers in the back of my mind.

This fear—this doesn't keep me from loving, but it does build a wall between me and loving someone openly, truly, and wholly. It's difficult to love someone completely with the "well, this person is going to die eventually" thought whispering menacingly to me as I look into someone's eyes. This would be like renovating your kitchen when you know your house is going to be demolished. It would seem pointless. You stop at a point, and you wonder if it's even worth it in the first place.

However, the only way you can truly love someone is if you are vulnerable with this person, and if you share yourself with them honestly and truly. The only way to truly know if someone can fit into your world is if you let them in—by sharing your truest thoughts, your fears, and your dreams. If you only let others near the periphery and never into your internal home, to put it bluntly, your home will always be empty, even if only in a metaphorical sense.

Even before all of this happened, I've had difficulties with this, and I've addressed this in previous essays. This is something I'm working on—on being honest with how I'm feeling, what I'm thinking, and how I'm processing the world around me with those I care for the most. The

only way you can truly build relationships with people is if you open yourself up fully, but this is difficult when you wonder if they're going to be there the next day. If this manic internal dialogue of *I wonder if they're going to be there the next day* is at the forefront, it's difficult to have any sort of those uneasy, but necessary conversations.

At times, to avoid these conversations, I hid myself, but this is something I'm actively working on. I need to work on addressing this in myself, addressing that I am worthy of love as I am—that I am good enough to be accepted by those around me, that they don't think I'm dumb or boring and that maybe they do want to spend time with me.

This is something I'm actively working on—I cannot continue to keep my emotions stuffed in a suitcase, ready to uproot at the moment of potential departure. I know this. This is not the kind of love that can grow because it's not sustainable, and I think for a while, I crafted it this way. I crafted it so I could pick up and leave, and I guarded myself from loving wholly because I deemed myself unworthy of love. If anything, as I mentioned before, this is how you get *stuck* in your own mind. You have to unlock these doors, you have to unpack your emotions, and you have to be open.

This was amplified when I lost Jake, and I lost his family at the same time. While admittedly I was always guarded around his family, which was of no fault of theirs, I saw how quickly they left (outside of his mom and his brother) and assumed if they could do it that quickly, so could everyone else. I stand by what I said in the first book—I understand it, truly. To them, I will always be tied to his memory. To them, because I did not let them truly get to know me, they knew me as his shadow. Literally. My nickname was *Shadow*.

Because Jake's personality was so amplified, I stand by that this probably would have happened to anyone he dated. He had a tendency to command the attention of the room—not intentionally, but simply because he was just that witty and charming. Just by being there and being himself, he became the center of the room. But especially since I didn't let my guard down, I never let them truly know me. For me, this *unknowing* was amplified simply by the walls I constructed.

But that aside, I went from seeing them at least once a month for some sort of birthday celebration to not seeing them at all, and knowing this was by design. With each Jake memorial I saw them post online, I knew I was left out intentionally. I know that at least one member of his family blames me for his death completely. Again, I want to address this makes sense to me as much as it can without agreeing with it, but I also want to address that I am human and that this hurt me.

It hurts to be rejected so suddenly, especially after knowing someone for so long. I also acknowledge that, no matter how much I'd like to, there's no way I can change this.

But it wasn't for lack of trying.

For a while, I forced myself to try to connect with his family again, to fit myself into a place I no longer fit. I remember specifically, two weeks after Jake's funeral, I pulled over on the side of a busy road to send someone in his family, someone I knew blamed me completely, a long message. I told him how great of a person Jake was, how great he was to me, and how terrible of a person I am.

I thought this self-deprecation would make him feel better, and maybe it did. I never got a response, so I will never know, and all of that is okay. That's his decision, and he has never been cruel to me, so it's okay. This is how he chose to move on, and what I've said previously is true—I do not hate him for that, I understand that, and I try not to dwell on that. And as I said before, you can't connect with everyone, and you can't make everyone happy without completely losing yourself.

This unsolicited proclamation of self-blame—I thought this would make them feel better, and I thought it would repair the relationship. But it only made me feel worse, and it gave what I truly believe is a false answer. I didn't believe it when I first said it—but I truly wanted them to have a place to put their blame, and I thought I would be able to give that as my parting gift to them, as the answer and the peace that they needed. But the more I said this, the more I internalized it, no matter how much I dwelled on it. It's possible that giving them a scapegoat gave them some immediate comfort, but again, I will never know. This was forced love—real love would have been honest, but because I was frantic, I tried to force them to accept me by knocking myself down to a place I knew I didn't belong.

I know this is common, that the family of the person you lost will either slowly or immediately try to lose contact. I understand the root of it, which keeps it from being in the center of my mind. I get it, but sometimes, this understanding brings the pain internal, rather than at an external scapegoat. A sustained, longing painful, rather than a simple stab of angry pain. Neither is more or less painful—it's just different. Sometimes I wish I hated them because maybe it'd be easier to be on one clear side of the spectrum. But I'm grateful that I do not hate them. I'm grateful that I still harbor positive memories with all of them. Though I do not harbor hatred, this does not heal the hurt of missing the people I grew to know through years of knowing Jake.

Now, I try to make a point to remember only the good times with his family. Much like the positive journaling I mentioned in previous essays, by only remembering good times, it is to cast this relationship in a new light. This light is not false, but true to a specific point in time—because this time together, despite our falling out, is still true, still real. To be hateful for this is to ignore the good times we had, and to unnecessarily bring myself down to a weaker, more hate-filled level. You have to try to look at them as Polaroids close to your heart—and these memories only change if you cast them into the shadows, knowing what you know now. You are in control of this, no matter how difficult it may be. You cannot force them to love you again, but also, they cannot force you to forget these positive memories, or to cast them into negative light. Only you can reshape these memories, and you have control over that, no matter how difficult it may seem.

And while I wish I could convince them to accept me again, I've had to learn that this is no longer possible.

This relationship will forever be different, but that doesn't make the past any more or less authentic than how I remember it.

Again, this book is not filled with answers—it is filled with things I am actively addressing and working on. I hope you are able to take something through me stating what I feel, even if it's not exactly the same.

For me, it helps when someone says how they are feeling if I can relate to it, learn from it—and I hope I've done the same for you.

Past his family, I had to learn to move on from Jake. At first, I harbored widowers guilt—the feeling that moving on from him is an assault to his memory. Every relationship seemed temporary to me because, in my mind, I cast him as my one true love, one that nobody else could aspire to. I forgot his flaws and held him on a pedestal. I saw others' flaws more readily because I was comparing them to this godlike figure I had constructed in my mind. I found myself dating people who didn't quite fit me simply because I didn't see a future with them—my mind was still locked on a future with Jake, no matter how impractical I acknowledged that was in my logical mind. I was wasting both of our time simply because I wasn't fully present.

This seems like the most natural place to apologize to everyone I've dated or tried to date in the past 2½ years, because I acknowledge I have not been the most present or the most open. To be clear, while I'm apologizing, this does not mean I think we should get back together, but I simply want to say I'm sorry.

Now that I've gotten that off my plate, I'll continue. Even as I was actively dating, I felt that dating someone new was an assault to Jake. That by loving someone new, I was staining his legacy and forgetting about him completely.

But this isn't true, and I acknowledge that this isn't true. If there is such thing as an afterlife, I am certain that Jake would want me find happiness because I know absolutely that he cared about me more than anyone I knew at the time, and that when he was in his right mind, he would want me to be happy.

But this didn't shake the feeling in my head.

It's difficult to remember this when I'm even *thinking* about building a future with someone else, knowing that he is incapable of doing the same thing. (Unless there's an afterlife. I have no idea. If there is, I hope he's finally dating those hypothetical Swedish twins he always talked about, and I hope they are just as witty and intelligent as he was—and if there is an afterlife, still is.)

But, while it may sound a bit callous to say, he's not here anymore, and I still am. If I want to truly move forward, I have to fully move forward. If I find someone to share this life with, awesome. And if I don't, that's okay, too, as long as it feels right to me. But not finding someone because I'm clinging to someone who has passed, because I'm too scared to fully move on—I will have no room to grow if I hold this in my heart.

For the most part, I've progressed past this. I cannot give a reason why—it happened so slowly, over the course of two years, naturally. As I started growing closer to other people, truly, Jake began to hold a different place in my heart. While he will always be there, I've been able to build more stable relationships without completely blocking his memory from my head. In these stable relationships, I feel I am actually honoring Jake—moving in the positive direction I know he'd want me to be.

I'm guessing it's not ideal for those I date, but I try to be honest about it. I've found that, by being honest about it, I learn whether this person truly is a good fit for me. It will forever be a part of me, so I've found it's best to be open about my past and address it as soon as possible in any relationship, as soon as it begins to get serious. It's difficult, and sometimes, relationships that seemed solid will suddenly evaporate, but it's better to know sooner rather than later.

Now, as I'm typing this, I've entered a new stage—the fear of losing the person you've grown to love again.

I believe there are limitless stages of love that I hope to experience with someone again one day. I do honestly believe I experienced these with Jake in our earlier years because we knew each other so well. I can truly say he was my best friend, even later, when we did not treat each other as we should have.

In our earlier years, we had true, honest, pure love. I am certain that I can find this with someone else, and while I know it won't be exactly the same, that's okay. I hope it will be equally as beautiful and as meaningful, and I know this is possible if I truly let it happen.

But it's letting myself be vulnerable enough for it to happen again.

When I seriously tried dating again, I carried a selfish love in my heart—I wanted someone there, and I wanted to make sure I wasn't alone.

Desperately, I fought to make sure I wasn't as alone as I felt, and I thought the only way this could happen is if I locked down a person to stay with. But once you truly connect with someone past surface interests, once you begin to share experiences and build memories together, feeling attached to this person is inevitable. This person becomes your *other*—your best friend, even if only for a while. Once I started to actually feel attached to and reliant upon this person, and once I began to plan even the shadow of a future, I immediately turned my mind to the potential of losing this person.

And I would run.

I knew I wasn't in a place to experience this loss again—I put my present self in a distant future, and that terrified me.

I often tell Petrina (you may remember her—my incredibly patient friend from the first book) that I want to date someone far younger than me because I'm scared to lose someone I love so intimately again like this. While usually I tell her this in jest, this is honest. I am truly fearful of another lover passing on before me, leaving me. I'm truly scared of being alone. Not that it's important to you as a reader, but I usually go for someone a few years older than me. For whatever reason, this seems to work the best for me. Knowing this, even thinking that I would date someone much younger than me shows where my head is at. "I cannot let this person die before me." This love—this love is a selfish love. Dating someone younger for reasons like this is no way to enter a relationship. I realize this.

I know I'm not ready for this pain yet, or even the anticipation of this pain, of looking into the eyes of the person I love the most knowing that one of us will die before the other.

I know I shouldn't think of this—I shouldn't avoid what will naturally happen to all of us. It's a part of the human condition. I should focus on the present, on finding someone who, if it does happen, will make even this most intense pain duller because I will have our memories to keep me company. I hope this person will show me another world I would have otherwise never experienced, and we will grow a world together that, even if this person passes before me, will still feel comfortable and warm to me.

The moments we will share will make it all worth it—and I know this because I often revisit memories with Jake with a fond heart. I know he made me a better person in the end. I am grateful for these memories, and there is no way in hell I would take any of them back, even knowing that it would eventually turn sour, and that he would eventually leave for good.

The reality is we are all here for a finite period of time. I am not immortal, nor you, nor anybody. This fear of death is like fearing a thunderstorm. At some point, it will happen. But that doesn't mean I should carry an umbrella and wear a raincoat on a perfectly sunny, summer day. I cannot retreat from sunshine because of the potential for rain. This fear—this is no way to live. Yes, we should be mindful of it, but it should not detract from the beauty in the beautiful moments. If anything, this inevitability should motivate us to make the most out of every moment—to breathe in the beautiful moments, to build upon these memories shared with the people we love the most. While I have not forgotten this pain, I should learn to move forward from it—to let others in, romantic or platonic, above all else.

I'm working on this.

Flowering from the Ashes

After experiencing significant loss, it can be easy to lose the will to enter the world again. For me, I was incredibly fragile, as I think anyone would be in this situation. When you're in this state, it's easy to retreat because that's what's comfortable to do. And that's okay to do, at first. There is a reason we do this instinctually. We need to give ourselves that time to cry, to mourn, to sleep, to rest. This is for the same reason deer retreat into their safe space in the woods after they've been injured — to heal and mend in a place they know is safe, unchanging.

At first, you *do* need to repair yourself. As long as you're able to do it healthfully, I think this retreat can, to a point, really help. Having days where you don't leave the house is okay, as long as you learn how to cope through these times. I think that's an incredibly powerful skill to have—to learn to manage on your own, in your own space.

It's also an important skill to know when you should ask for help, and when to know it is time to reenter the world. It's important to know when you are able to take care of something yourself, but it's just as important as recognizing when you need to ask for help. Soon, I hope asking for help will be just as easy as retreating when I need to. I'm still working on this, but I hope to get to a point where it comes naturally, where I don't feel like a burden asking for help when I truly need it. And, I can tell you from personal experience that usually, once you open up, people *want* to help.

For me, while I was at my lowest, my worst traits reared their heads and made their presence known—it was by lying, by my inability to set boundaries for myself, by retreating behind a persona to protect myself from my own self-constructed demons. While this was exacerbated by trauma, these unhealthy coping mechanisms were brought in from my past life—things I never addressed even before any of this happened, before I had been able to hide them. Now, they were impossible to ignore.

Trauma does that—at least for me, it pulled my worst traits to center stage.

At first, these traits were the fuel for my manic quest for reason—and I tried to hide them through constant motion. But once I stopped moving and I still saw them there, it made it easier to identify. Instead of allowing these flaws to simmer in the background, where they had been before, I'm fortunate that I kept them in the front, and I began to combat them. This is an ongoing process, as I have to backtrack, find their roots (mostly insecurity), and address deep below the surface. What doesn't kill you makes you stronger, but that only happens if you actually work on getting stronger. Unfortunately, you can't build a six-pack without working on it, no matter how nice that would be.

For Personal or external reasons—an argument For Both

Improving for Yourself

At first, I tried to be the best version of myself, so I tried to continue applying advice that Jake had given me as I was before to who I grew into now—as if he was still here giving me that same advice. This created a glass ceiling for my recovery. As much as I would still love to hear advice from him, no matter how otherworldly and eerie that would be, I know I can't.

Despite knowing that this advice no longer applied to my new life logically, I clung to this emotionally. As I grew, Jake's advice did not. I clung to who I was with him, and to the advice he gave me at that time, as a way to preserve his memory. An example of this would be one he showed me through his actions—he was an incredibly motivated, incredibly strong-willed person. And at a certain point in my life, this was good for me because it motivated me to give my 100%, to preserve his legacy. However, this need to give 100% all the time drove me to obsessively chase an unobtainable goal of total perfection, which, if he was here now, I'm sure he would have checked me on. But he's not here anymore to do that, so I took his example and drove it to the extreme—a "this is what he would have wanted me to do."

I had to learn to see his advice as fallible, not all-encompassing. This can be difficult after a person passes, because for whatever reason (even if you're mindful of it), it's easy to put the person on an infallible pedestal, if anything, to maintain his or her memory in your mind. It's easy to forget that the person who passed was also human.

While a lot of his advice was great, and while some of it is still very applicable, I realize now that I had to start rebuilding past the advice he gave me. This was a difficult hurdle for me to jump over—addressing that he is no longer here, and that I have grown past the person I was with him.

As I began to work on what I knew were problems when Jake was alive (mostly because he called me out on it constantly, which again, I stand by—this was a good, selfless thing, and you should always challenge your partner), I began to work toward self-improvement. It is still in the back of my mind that I need to improve for Jake, but now, it's also a daily practice for me, past his memory. I had to address that he is no longer here, and I still am.

I've found that keeping a daily journal helps, if only to force myself to reflect on my day. Writing helps assess how I'm truly feeling, and how I can improve, and it helps me touch on what I've done well that day. It is a mindful meditation, an internal checkup to make sure I'm living as I know I should be—for myself and for others. I try to keep it as positive as possible. For me, self-deprecation was a mask I used to justify my faults, but I've noticed that once I'm more positive about myself, goals seem much easier to accomplish. I check myself more naturally when I acknowledge the things I'm doing right because I'm encouraging them—when I spend more time focusing on what I'm doing right, what I'm doing wrong tends to take a back seat, and honestly, tends to happen less often. When I'm focusing on what I'm doing wrong, it perpetuates the cycle by bringing me down to an unnecessarily low level. I've learned that, for me, when I'm positive, I encourage myself to *continue* living more positively. With it, I truly believe that when I carry confidence, I can achieve anything.

While often I still go back to Jake's advice, I do not hold it as my Ten Commandments, as I had before. They are simply, now, memories of his philosophies that I can still tie into my own life—not chains I should hold myself to. I see them, now, as dynamic, rather than laws to uphold to maintain his legacy.

These were all things I knew I needed to do, for me, for my happiness, for my well-being.

Telling Your Story

We are naturally communal, so to care about your total well-being, it's also important to think of how your actions impact who you respect most. That outside view—this is the most valuable thing we have as humans. If the people sharing their views with you care about you, they will want to see you at peace with yourself, and they will let you know when they're worried. They will be there for you when you need them, when they are able to be present; you should do the same. This is a give and take, a balance that, when you find the right people, should happen naturally. These communities we build as we grow older—they're important. To truly be present in this world, you have to interact with it, past your own personal perspective.

To everyone who truly knows you, they can see these deviations much more readily than you can—they're looking right at you, and they don't have the clutter of inner thoughts that you have in your brain every day. They see the portrait of you at that point, and they are able to associate it with a photo book of memories past—easily comparable to them. (Much like how you notice how long someone's hair has grown after you haven't seen them in six months.) They are able to detect the subtle changes that build over time that you may not be able to realize. Through the tunnel vision of trying to make sure everyone thought I was okay, I neglected everything else that mattered. I canceled plans. I forgot about plans. My jokes turned from natural to manic, which was far more obvious to those I truly knew than I previously realized. I like to think I'm a pretty funny lady, but only when I'm being truly honest with myself—and much like nearly everything else in life, if it's forced or untrue, it's never as good as the real stuff. People let me know, but I chose to ignore them. I justified that they didn't truly know me, but I

didn't realize that they *did* know me, outside of my internal thoughts. It's a different kind of knowing, and it's no more or less authentic than your own self-image.

It wasn't until I started truly interacting with people again, wholly and honestly, that I was able to escape my head. Once I started listening to advice, truly talking with others, I felt less lonely. It was easier to motivate myself to rebuild.

While writing my first book, I struggled with thinking, "Why am I sharing this story? Why would anyone care?" Most of my early drafts were ditched not because I thought they sucked, but mostly because I felt that telling my story would be a worthless endeavor—another memoir in a growing pile of memoirs that hit the shelves every day. I assumed that my life was boring, that my story was boring, and that nobody would find anything in it. Somehow, despite my nagging thoughts, I still found the gusto to write it. And I'm incredibly glad I did.

While looking back, I do think there were a few points I could have written better, I really, truly would never take back writing my first book. If anything, I hope that it makes people understand that they don't have to hold it in—that they can tell their stories, no matter how rough they are, and they can make something from them. Maybe even better than mine. However, truly, saying one story is better than the other is ridiculous—all stories are different and powerful, as long as it is an honest portrayal.

My favorite part of every signing is when people come up to me and share their stories. This exchange of stories—open and honest—is what makes every minute of this experience worth it. Often, simply because of the subject the book deals with, people who previously had no idea what the book was about will open up to me about their struggles, what they have encountered, and what they are doing to try to build from their own unique rubbles. This exchange helps me reevaluate how I'm coping with my own trauma, and I hope my story can do the same for others. I think it's the right time for this in our culture—like so many other things, we're realizing that sometimes it's better to talk about things rather than ignore the elephants in the room.

It also is telling that so many people *truly want* to talk about it, but feel they need to have that specific safe space to talk. And I get that, completely. That was the entire point of my first book—I never felt like I could talk about it because I feared that doing so would be a burden to those around me, and that they would get what I felt was "unnecessarily worried about me." Because I didn't give myself the time to find my own safe space, I harbored these thoughts within—I shouldered them on my own.

Obviously, as you could tell from my first book, I totally had it under control. Completely. 100% had it in the bag, you guys. Conquered that grief. Nobody had to worry for a minute about me.

(I hope you realize I'm joking. I realize I was a mess, and I'm fortunate that I found the strength to pull myself out, with the help of those I care about the most.)

Especially where I'm from—the Midwest, borderline rustbelt (Milwaukee)—being open and honest about how you're feeling is often seen as a weakness. While nobody would ever say that openly (we're *far* too repressed for that), it's telling that where I'm from, it's taboo to see a therapist. When you're seeing a therapist, the common response is, "Are you okay?" or simply "Why?" Where I'm from, the stoic repression of emotions is seen as a strength, not something that could actually hurt you in the long run. I don't think this is unique to Milwaukee, though it may manifest in different ways in different cities.

One thing I have struggled with whenever someone asks what my first book is about—I soften the actual premise. I usually say, "After my boyfriend passed, I went on a series of road trips following the last band we saw together." I feel, by saying that he simply passed, by keeping it vague, this shelters the person from an awkward or uncomfortable experience. But there's always the awkward and inevitable, "Oh, I'm so sorry. How did he pass?" where I then have to say it anyway. I still have to say, "Suicide." I usually try to soften the blow with saying, "He was always so self-sufficient," which I've learned is a very dark joke for someone who has just been surprised with that sort of information. This does not soften the blow, at all, ever, but for whatever reason, it always feels like the right thing to say there. It never is the right thing to say. Ever.

It wasn't until I was speaking with the head of NAMI Boston about my flyer for a signing in their city. Point blank, she asked, "If this is about suicide, why don't you say anything about it?" We had talked extensively over the phone and email about being honest about our stories, and by her calling me out on this, I immediately realized that *she was right*. While I had made it a point to be honest about everything else, I still felt the need to shelter others from the entire premise of my book. Obviously, they would find out eventually if they bought my book. Past that, in order to own my story, I had to actually *tell* it. *All* of it.

One of my favorite books is Elaine Scarry's *On Beauty and Being Just*, where she explains that true art comes from deep within the soul, authentic and pure. The more times it's copied and transposed on its surface, the more it loses its integrity. With each surface-level deviation I made on top of my life story, it lost its shine, which made me think I simply wasn't interesting when my false story didn't resonate. I didn't realize that it was worth telling simply because I transposed it and copied surface-level details—it wasn't interesting because I was too scared to show my soul, too scared to actually tell the truth.

One thing I've been working on this year is owning my own story—even its darkest recesses. This goes beyond the entire Jake story, to my deepest other stories, as everyone has. These stories that build our morals and shape the way we see the world—often times, they're learned the hard way, and sometimes opening up about them is a good way to process how you choose to react to these deeper, darker moments. Often times, people who have had similar stories react to them in different ways. And often times, you can learn from these reactions.

I would never go out of my way to tell people that my boyfriend committed suicide, unsolicited. If it is explicitly asked, I should own it as best I can. If anything, if they purchase the book, they're going to find out what happened anyway. It's not the most subtle about what happened—it's pretty to the point.

However, if you're shouting it to a room full of people who don't know you, unsolicited, you obviously haven't fully come to terms with it in your head. You need to open this topic internally and externally—you can't expect others to figure out your problems for you, especially if

you sneak-attack them with problems at level 11. You have to accept it yourself before you can expect others to; any other way simply wouldn't be fair, especially because they will never fully know the story better than you.

Above all else, you should be open about your story. You should be true to yourself. However, you should also learn to process your story, both internally and externally. Simply telling your story—that's only half the battle. It's learning how to truly *own* your story before you expect others to own and accept it themselves.

Once I was able to begin to clear these blocks out of my head, I found that I actually enjoyed sharing my story—but even past that, I enjoyed leaving my apartment again. I enjoyed returning to the things in life that I previously enjoyed. I looked forward to going to a show, out to dinner, or for a walk with friends. I found that once I wasn't creating a performance every time I left my house, there was so much less stress. Once I began to be honest with myself, I could have fun again. I could really live again.

Building Beyond the Person You Lost (Without Blocking Them Out)

For so long, everything about moving on felt taboo. I mentioned this before, but want to touch on it again.

I felt that, to grieve properly, I needed to cling to him to retain his memory. As I mentioned in the first book, I thought this meant physically visiting his grave. This is something I'm still not able to do.

I thought this meant that, for the rest of my days, I wasn't allowed to date, because if I moved on, this meant (in my mind) that I was moving on from him, forgetting about him.

With time, I've learned this is not the case. To be a functioning human being, you cannot continue to cling to your past, no matter what your past is. You have to keep challenging yourself. You have to accept that desire to go out into the world and accept love again—for yourself and from others.

The thing was, at first, when I recognized I was feeling better again, I forced myself to feel worse—a never-ending, self-loathing cycle. As humans, we all experience light and darkness; even in our darkest moments, a good bowl of perfectly cinnamon-ed oatmeal can bring us joy, if only for a minute. For me, at a certain point in my grieving, I would mentally self-flagellate myself every time I felt any sort of happiness until I was back to my lowest point again. In my mind, if I were to feel happy at all, this meant that I wasn't sad enough, that I hadn't cared enough about him when I knew he felt nothing, when I knew that he had suffered. In effect, I was extending the last part of his legacy. It was extreme pain. I carried on this pain for him—though I know if he was here, this isn't what he'd want me to do.

I clung to the idea that I needed to make everything better—that I needed to right all wrongs—for too long. This held up my recovery process because I was so hyper-focused on making sure everyone else was okay without making sure *I* was okay. This manifested itself outside of those I encountered at home, my stable relationships, to those I met during my travels. If I sensed even the smallest amount of discomfort, I would go to great lengths to make sure that they felt okay even when I felt awful.

It always seems easier to care for others than to care for yourself because once people are out of sight, they have to deal with their problems on their own. But caring for yourself? You are with yourself all the time. If you hurt, you cannot walk away from that. The only way you can move forward is self-care; otherwise, you get stuck in that pain. Caring for others above yourself is pious, and what we are told is the true ideal of how to be a functioning member of society. And absolutely, you should help other people—I believe it is the most powerful form of therapy. But it must be balanced with taking care of yourself. You cannot reach out to someone from the bottom of the well, or if you're both there, a hug at the bottom of the well doesn't get you back to the top. The only way you can really help someone is if *you* are in a good place. You cannot give yourself wholly if you're not whole yourself.

It wasn't until I cut myself a break that I truly began to be a good person. In some ways, on the surface, the ways I did this made me look like a bad person. I stopped volunteering so much. I stopped going out as much. My social circle grew smaller. I spent more time on myself, time I used to spend on others.

With every night I spent with a cheap Egyptian clay face mask re-reading the same Guy Delisle graphic novel—the one on Jerusalem—my mind unwound from what I should be doing to what I am *currently* doing. By appreciating the present, I'm able to be more present than I was before. Because my brain was relaxed rather than wired on "I should be doing something," it worked better.

Before, I was hyper-focused on being a good person. I made sure that if someone needed help, I was the first line of defense. Even if I wasn't the right person for the job, I would force myself to be, even if I didn't have the time or the mentality necessary for it. One of many examples of this would be when I took a remote editing job for an online women's interest magazine—I was editing a slew of articles each week on topics I had no interest in, such as, "Which tampons are the best for those with wide cervixes?" and "What balayage hairstyle best fits your unique personality?" and "What to do if your man still hasn't popped the question?". I couldn't do a good job because, simply, I did not give a shit about what I was doing, but I convinced myself it's what I *should* be doing. (I ended up getting fired from this job, the first and only time I was ever fired, which was probably for the best, to be honest.)

I was wired to think that I should be doing something at all times, and this job was *something*, even though it wasn't necessarily enjoyable or the best use of my time. I wasn't comfortable when my plate wasn't full, mostly because then I had time to think about what I truly should be doing, instead of some other *something* to fill my time. The list could go on and on with examples of this, but this is the one that comes to mind first.

I would sacrifice my own personal life to ensure others could have theirs, because in my mind, they deserved it more than I did. In my mind, I could handle it; therefore, I should do it. When I heard others complain about how busy they were, I would focus on how to alleviate that stress rather than thinking about how stressed this would make

me. I never stopped to think about when I would get a break—I was hyper-focused on making sure everyone else got theirs.

Granted, my break from this was forced. After Jake died, there was no way I could continue this work regimen because I wasn't able to do as much—at first, I was in inpatient, where I literally didn't have access to the outside world, and I was unable to work or to communicate with those outside of the hospital. Past that, depression kept me from leaving my apartment, or even my bed. I wasn't able to make the connections necessary to keep my plate full.

As I mentioned previously, I had an excellent therapist while in inpatient who taught me that many of my emotions are normal, and that I should analyze them as I feel them. For as long as I can remember, I've struggled with anxiety, which is a double-edged sword. This drove me to constantly be working on something—convincing myself that if I'm not doing something, I'm not doing anything, and that I'm worthless. I was used to working at 100% for so long because I was driven by my anxiety and that fear of being worthless, so I was used to the stress that accompanied this.

She explained to me that those suffering with anxiety disorders are used to operating at a "cup-near-overflowing" level—a level far past what a normal person would consider "overwhelming" simply because we're used to being overwhelmed by even the most minute aspects of life. This makes me sound superhuman, but also you have to consider that those who are not suffering from an anxiety disorder still have room left in their cup if they add any sort of stress in their lives. If you are only operating at 75%, you still have room in your cup if you realize you have to fill up your gas tank even if you have to be downtown in 15 minutes—meaning you will not have an anxiety attack at a seemingly small inconvenience. Because the average mind still allows itself room for more stresses, the anxious mind forces me to work at 100%, which does not allow for any unexpected deviations. Everything has to work exactly as I plan it to; otherwise, I melt down. My cup would immediately overflow, and I wouldn't be able to contain it with even the smallest deviation.

Because operating at 75% is not normal for me, I've had to force myself to relax once in a while. It's been difficult for me to realize that sometimes the best thing I can do for others is to care for myself. When operating at 100% all of the time, even self-care is enough to throw me into an anxiety attack (which, obviously, turned into more anxiety as things built up in my apartment, like laundry and dishes). I didn't give myself time to take care of the things I needed so I could care for myself, so because I was hyper-focused on helping everyone else, my ability to truly help people dwindled. If you're only half present, it's near impossible to truly help someone, as I wanted to do—or to help yourself, as I should have been doing, simply because your brain is not working at its full potential. You will never be your best version if you're constantly working at 100%, if you're moving from one anxiety attack to another. If you do not stop to care for yourself—if you do not spend a few days at a 50% anxiety level, serenading your cats with and dancing along to a Sonny Cleveland album in your living room (or whatever it is you do when you're trying to unwind)—you will ultimately suffer.

As I've mentioned in previous essays, I've forced myself to take a walk every day. This helps to unwind my mind—it's a set time where I don't have to do anything except move forward and meditate on what I will be doing that day. For me, this is a daily treat I give myself. It seems small, but in the past, I would have simply woken up and gone to work right away—immediately diving into the things I have to do for other people instead of doing something for myself. But because I start the day for me, this builds context onto the rest of my day. I'm mentally

clearer because I took the time to care for myself first thing, rather than putting it off for later (then inevitably procrastinating on self-care).

And it's difficult—it's difficult to fully process that, to be a good person, you do need to spend time caring for yourself. For me, this didn't process until I started helping others with a well-rested brain, rather than one wracked with thinking "I should be doing all of these things because I should be doing things." Doing good comes more naturally when you *feel* good. Instead of simply being another task to accomplish, it's easier to help someone truly if your mind is in it. It can't truly be "in it" if you aren't fully focused, aren't fully there.

To me, it still feels odd to say, "The only way you can be a good person is if you first take care of yourself." I still suffer with the thoughts of "I should be doing something for others, because I'm strong and I can handle these stresses better." (And this may or may not be true—I can only speak from my own personal feelings; therefore, I have no idea how others process these stresses).

By admitting that, possibly, maybe, I can feel better if I choose to take care of myself while still caring for others, I've found I feel more rested on the same amount of sleep. By caring for myself, I'm learning to love myself as much as I love and respect those around me, those I want to help. And I realized that I, too, was worthy of being helped, and that what I was doing was also great (at least, if I spent the time necessary to cultivate my own projects, rather than wondering how I could help others with theirs.) I've learned how to respect myself while still respecting those around me—a balance I have to work on, but with each day, it seems to come more naturally. I'm able to be influenced by others simply because I'm working on myself and with others—and this encourages me, and help keeps me grounded.

The Fight

The moment I decided to write this second book, I debated whether I would include this. It's an incredibly sensitive discussion that really lays myself bare in front of people who, I feel, ultimately would not understand it and would immediately vilify me once they read it.

But the point of this book is to move forward, and to do that, I have to accept the entire story and lay it bare in front of all of you as readers, no matter how you may interpret it. I cannot hide it from you anymore if I want to healthfully move forward.

I cheated on him.

I'm not proud of it, and if I had been in the same situation again, in my current mind, of course it wouldn't have happened.

But it did.

For so long, I hid from this, but it would inevitably come out as my conscience lured it out—even if it was only myself, wracked by guilt, with harsh light casting down on my sleep-deprived face in my bathroom mirror at

2:00 am. My body was exhausted, but my mind would re-live the decisions leading up to this. I never thought that I would ever forgive myself for these weak moments leading up to these decisions. But I have. Slowly, but surely, I have.

I do not condone my actions. I admit they were the actions of a weak character. I am fortunate that I have grown past this weak character. However, I do feel since you have been with me for this long, I owe you at least this much to tell you this very intimate detail. And I feel the only way to continue to build away from this is to admit what I did wrong, to acknowledge it as openly as I can, and learn to move forward from there in a more positive direction.

But let me explain how I got to this point.

We were not perfect. Neither of us. It's often said that broken people will find each other, but when we found each other, we were not broken. We were too young to be fully broken—at 17, you own the world, even if the world isn't going exactly the way you want it to. In these first few years, we shared everything—jokes, dreams, and lots and lots of coffee and breakfast sandwiches.

But as we got older, we did not adjust our relationship to fit our newfound worldviews. Separately, we became broken. We tried to hide this from each other. He—he was dealing with he early stages of bipolar. Me—I was dealing with poor self-esteem issues that I've harbored since a child, and the need to make everyone around me happy before myself.

It's difficult to be in a relationship with someone who is slowly losing his mind, but equally difficult to be with someone who is constantly battling self-esteem issues. And my issues were much more deep seeded—they weren't the external "I feel fat today," at all. They were of my self-worth, feeling worthless, feeling useless. As soon as you feel those things, you do not seek out healthy relationships. You seek out temporary relationships because ultimately, you do not see yourself worthy of love. You break it off before you have to deal with anything—that is at least how I manufactured it in my mind, even if I didn't realize this at the time.

But with Jake, above everything else, he was my best friend. My confidant. And even though he was my confidant, I hid this from him. I respected him so much that I did not want any chance of losing him, so I pretended everything was going great while harboring a separate life to keep myself going, to try to build a solid base out of eggshells. And I admit it seems strange to say "I respected him" while also going behind his back, but when the mind is frantic, these now-obvious connections didn't seem obvious at the time. My mind was on self-preservation—it was finding any sort of stability in an otherwise unstable condition.

When I realized I couldn't make him happy, instead of sitting down and having the very necessary discussion I should have had, I fled and sought shelter with someone else. I felt guilty asking him to do this for me because in my eyes, I was not worthy of this from him.

I held him on a pedestal for so long, and I think at least for the beginning of our relationship, he deserved it. He was an incredibly strong person, with quick wit and a kind heart. Again, I don't want to speak for him, but I believe he did the same for me. We adored each other, and in those first few years, we knew each other more intimately than I've known anyone. When I realized that this pedestal was flawed, that I had crafted him into some godly figure instead of the very human figure that he was, I was scared. I blamed myself. Instead of retreating, he lashed out because he saw I wasn't living up to the potential he saw for me in his mind. (At least, that's how I interpret it, now. Again, I can't speak for him.)

I flaked, to put it lightly and bluntly.

The worst part is that he found out not from me, but from reading my diary.

This part—this is something I will never forgive myself for, and I actually think that's a good thing because hopefully, that will ensure that I am never in this situation again. I think this was, again, the actions of a weak character, but also actions that cannot be condoned. Even after it happened, I realized I couldn't keep it from him forever. But time seems to go on for an eternity until it doesn't.

Time is finite. I waited for the right time to tell him, but obviously, with this kind of thing, there is no "right time."

There is never a right time for tough conversations, which I think is what makes them the most difficult to have. What is most difficult to realize when you're trying to find the perfect time to tell something to anyone is you don't have time—the longer you wait, the longer it festers in your mind. And the more secrets you keep to cover up this initial lie.

But I hope by admitting it, I can give a very human face to a very humanly weak decision. I hope that you can learn from what I did and apply it to your own relationships. Even if it's spilling wine on your brand-new white carpet—your partner is going to find out eventually. Even if it's feeding the wrong food to your best friend's dog while she is on vacation—it'll come up eventually if that dog is truly as sensitive

as she says it is. The strongest thing you can do is to take a deep breath and admit what you did wrong—to confess without defenses up, to be vulnerable in front of your partner or whoever it is you wronged. It's terrifying, and many times, the actions leading to this are incredibly flawed, but these flaws are human and cannot be avoided. They only fester more the longer they are pushed to the side. And it's possible they may reject you, and this is terrifying, too—I know firsthand because it was this very fear of rejection that kept me from admitting my wrongs to Jake.

But at least you have the peace of mind that you were honest and sincere leading up to it. Life is vulnerable, visceral, and entirely too short to spend it hiding secrets from those you care about—even if your secrets contain your flaws. Those who love you love you fully, but they can only love you fully if you *give* yourself fully, honestly, truly. You owe this to them.

While I have forgiven myself for this, it does not mean I do not still regret this. I do—wholly. I regret that I involved people who should not have been involved in the first place. I regret what I did to him. But I cannot continue to self-flagellate with self-deprecating thoughts. I cannot continue to live in the past and to continue to hate myself for these actions.

I have to move forward from this simply by learning, and by promising myself to do better going forward. The person I know I can and should be. The person I have become.

Healing The Stigma

Let me get one thing as honest and as clear as possible—after I've opened up about what has happened to me, I am not allowed to have a sad day, ever, without a few people growing concerned that I'm regressing. I'm not allowed to have a bad day, a sad day, or even a mediocre day. Even though I went into this with minor, manageable depression, that has been wiped clean from everyone's memory after 2016. Every sad day is connected to Jake now, though many times it has nothing to do with him. Even if it's just "I'm sad because I didn't get enough sleep last night and I'm also sad that there are no peanut butter cups in my house," it's difficult to convince people that you're okay unless you're happy 100% all of the time. You are now on a *sadness pedestal* that some people are now convinced they cannot reach, and can never understand. Because I faced an admittedly horrific tragedy, this tends to alienate some people who I once held close.

That's okay, and I've grown to accept that and move forward.

Though I've moved past it, I also want to say that for the average person, nobody is happy 100% of the time. Most of the time, we're decent, which there's nothing wrong with. In fact, right now, I'm going on a crusade to rebrand *decent* as a perfectly acceptable mood to be in because it's honest and it's homeostasis and it's humble. But for some people, they want you to be *better* than good. They want you to be *great*. And while their heart is in the right place, this just sometimes isn't completely possible. And to be honest, it's not something I would want for myself. To be perfectly honest with you, being great 100% of the time sounds exhausting.

This can be frustrating, especially as someone who is often told to "smile more." And this was even before 2016—when I was in Germany in 2011 visiting Jake, who was studying in Frankfurt for a year, I had an old man yell at me in German for not smiling on Christmas, probably something akin to *Lachle mehr!* , which is the last thing I want to hear in any context, even if it has to be translated to me.

I was actually in a great mood at the time. I was over the moon about seeing the love of my life after a six-month break in a new country, excited to see his new world, excited to experience it with him for a month. That didn't matter. (I guess my face tends to scream *not happy*, no matter what my mood is.)

This has caused me to lie about how I'm feeling—to instead say, "I'm great!" even if I felt like a sack of shit that fell out of the back of a Toyota Yaris that was then was run over by a semi-truck, and that then hit the cement divider on the highway in one dramatic, defeated splat. Even *then*, I would fake a smile and pretend like everything was great. This is exactly what I'm trying to avoid doing now, as this mood repression is what fueled my manic quest for reason in 2017.

For me, blunt honesty is what I need, but this is not the way to approach everyone. This is not the way to tell everyone how you feel, which sucks, but it's honest. There is a way to be honest with those who may treat you differently, though, much like my rebranding of *decent*—it's to put it in a different light.

You cannot expect someone to understand your hurt if you do not give the entire picture, and if you attack that person with your pain. Like I mentioned before, by honestly sharing and letting your vulnerabilities show, and by being open to suggestions and discussion, this tends to help me explain how I am feeling to people without that wall of tragedy covering my words. Sometimes, this internal rebranding as I'm talking with others helps me process it in my own mind. If I cast it in a new light instead of exposing it in its raw, gritty, unprocessed form—if I process my thoughts internally before I let them out externally—I've found I'm able to connect with people much better, despite that wall.

Of course, nobody can fully understand your pain because they are not living in your brain—they can never know the nuances as well as you do unless you lay them out.

This obviously does not work for everyone—not everyone will understand your hardships, especially if you haven't completely processed them in your brain yourself. That's okay. It's difficult—I'm not saying it's not. And, again, I feel like I sound like a broken record

when I say, "It's okay," but I mean it. *It's okay*. It's better than pretending to be okay and shouldering this burden yourself.

With that stigma that surrounds those who have openly struggled, or those who have experienced tragedy—at times, I've kept what has happened to me, for fear of how others will react. For me, especially because I am trying to rebuild my world outside of my struggle and my book, it's difficult when someone finds out what I'm doing through word of mouth or through a flyer—suddenly, that dynamic changes.

Those who have suffered have time to process those struggles in their minds. Those who have not experienced those struggles have not had time to process—so it makes sense for them to suddenly feel nervous or confused.

That dynamic always changes once someone figures out what happened, which is natural, because all of us put ourselves in someone else's shoes when we hear about their struggles. And foreign struggles always seem worse when happening to someone else—when you're not the one suffering from them, when you're not the one who has experienced them firsthand.

This dynamic shift is human. Those around you—there's no way they can understand your pain or how you deal with that. If they are trying to make you feel better, even if it doesn't work, you should acknowledge that their heart is in the right place and try to better explain what works for you in the future, instead of cutting them out completely, as I did to some of those in my life. This is something I will probably never forgive myself for, in my weakest days, but I have moved past it and I have learned from it—some of these relationships I can't rebuild, but I've luckily been able to learn from that. Fortunately, not everyone has been through the same things I have been through, so I've had a lot of these encounters.

This is what makes us human—our need to connect and to help those around us, to build our relationships around us. Instead of seeing someone as ignorant, see it as vulnerable and human, while still exposing them to how you feel respectfully. Remember that by reaching out to you, they are putting themselves in a vulnerable position as well.

I completely get it—this is something I used to do. I used to be the person to ask, "But are you okay, *really*?" To be clear, I do not hate the people who do this, but at the same time, it does make me feel uncomfortable. However, it has to be addressed that those who are reaching out to you feel equally uncomfortable. Much like they can't read your mind, you also cannot read theirs.

You are not your past. You are who you are, present. Unless you cling to your past, you are your present self, and only you can define yourself. But you cannot expect those around you to understand this immediately—this is something you have to explain to them.

Don't shut them out—guide them on how they can help. Remove that stigma by actively showing others how to.

"What should I say to someone who has lost someone to suicide?

This is the most common question I've been asked after writing my first book—and the one I feel is the most difficult to answer. I want to reiterate that everyone is different, that everyone processes everything differently, and that what worked for me may not work for your niece, your best friend, or whoever else you're wondering on how to approach.

In my opinion, the emphasis shouldn't be on what you say to them. You should only say something if they bring it up to you, and to simply be a vessel for listening, rather than trying to offer advice. At least for me, when I was in the peak of processing, the last thing I wanted to do was to re-live the trauma while in public. If I finally pulled myself out of my apartment, that meant I was looking for an escape. I didn't want to rehash my traumas; the few times I did, I would bring it up first (even when I didn't know how to, or even when it was awkward). When I did want to talk about it, I would.

The emphasis shouldn't be on getting them to talk about it—it should be about knowing that if they want to talk about it, you're there for them, wholly. Support is the most important thing during these times, as well as reminding those who are suffering that there is a world outside of their trauma. Be kind to them—include them in plans, knowing fully that they may cancel last-minute if they're having a rough day. Don't hate them for it if they do, or if they do ghost, the emphasis should be on letting them know they aren't abandoned.

After Jake passed the way he did, I feared that if he could leave that suddenly, my other relationships would, too. I started to process my relationships differently, assuming that everyone would leave eventually. My closest friends now are not the ones who asked me how I was doing on a daily basis. My closest friends were the ones who would send me stupid cat memes, who would rehash embarrassing memories we've shared together, or would talk with me about their crushes, just

as they had before. Those people didn't change—they were reminders that I still had solid, unwavering relationships out there, rather than a dynamic shift.

It's difficult—I get it. In these situations, I tend to mother-hen, to smother, to try to fix all of the problems for this person. There is no simple fix to an incredibly complex situation like this—there are so many different aspects associated with it, which makes it difficult to truly understand the situation. You can't give answers without knowing the situation fully, and there's no way you can ever know the situation as completely as the person who is suffering. For me, it was this trauma, and I was also dealing with the aftermath of what was, on both sides, a very unhealthy relationship. There is no way anyone could have known about this simply because I hadn't told anyone, so any advice people would give to me unsolicited always seemed forced because it wasn't fully grasping the entire situation. It didn't seem applicable because I didn't feel comfortable giving them all of the information, at least not at that time.

There were often times I felt pressured to talk with people about it, simply because they asked about it and I could tell they wanted me to talk about it. I found myself faking emotions I knew they felt I should process at that time, based off of what I knew they expected me to feel. But much like any instance in life, when you're actually going through something, often times the processing stage is much different than you could have ever anticipated. And the only way to process it is simply by going through it. I never hated anyone for trying to anticipate how I was processing this incredibly traumatic situation, but it did make me feel alienated when I felt others were putting me on a trauma pedestal. It was hard—the only thing I truly needed at that time was to be included, to be accepted, to be told, "That sucks, but the rest of your world is still there, and that's not changing anytime soon."

Again, I understand this question, and I understand this question comes from a good place. The one thing I want to emphasize is that neither of us know what to do. There is no answer on how to feel better because there *is* no way to feel better in this incredibly traumatic situation. The best thing you can say? "That sucks," followed by consistently supporting

them as you had before. An unchanging approach to the relationship is far more impactful than any words could say. The world of this person has just been rocked in a way that is difficult to comprehend, meaning any sort of personal familiarities will help this person realize that there is a world outside of trauma. Even if it's taking that person to her favorite restaurant for free chips and salsa—often times, any sort of reminder that there is a world outside of trauma is the best thing you can do for someone who has been through something similar.

I'm speaking for what was best for me. Again, this could be different for your niece, your sister-in-law, your friend. But for me, any sort of reminder of the world outside of myself was what I needed. When others hyper-focused on that trauma, that was when I felt trapped, when I felt the need to retreat. But it was when others took me for walks in parks I've been talking about visiting but never have, or sent me stupid articles from *The Onion*, or invited me to comedy shows, all while being patient if I was having a difficult day and canceled—this unchanging support was much more powerful than anything anyone could have ever said to me.

Epilogue

Here, now. March 24, 2019. In three weeks, I will be completely done with my tour with book one, and I'm finally starting to understand how to organize a tour on my own. I'm finally starting to fully learn how to own my story authentically, rather than as a set story I wrote in 2018, rather than distancing it as something that had happened in my past. I'm finally starting to understand that the story I wrote last year is dynamic, ever-changing, and that it will continue to build as I continue to process. I've learned how to share this with others—with those I cherish the most, and with those I've just met.

I had hoped that once the tour ended, I would be able to distance myself from it, that I would move on from it fully—but as I'm learning in these last few stops, that's never going to be the case. It will *always* be a part of me. It will continue to be a part of both my private and public life, and I'm learning how to mesh that into my life moving ahead, sustainably and productively. The purpose of this book is to describe how I'm moving forward—and much like my first book, this one will also continue to grow, far beyond these final pages.

In my last book, I told you about the cut and burn I got on my arm—a scar of Rush's *Snakes and Arrows* tour symbol. While my scar artist has assured me it is still healing healthfully, the process has been delayed by hypertrophic scarring (if you Google it, the images look far worse than mine do, but it's still not exactly friendly for short sleeves). It's funny—my mom had a scar on her leg that started to hypertrophic scar. Apparently, it's something that runs in our family (excess collagen buildup with particularly traumatic injuries, whether they're self-induced or by some camping accident, like with my mom's). And from what I've seen, this doesn't happen often. I'm part of a small percentage of potential side effects.

Much in my last book, I'll overanalyze this attribute of mine. I had said my scar would heal within the year, but unexpectedly, it grew and morphed into something else. My scar artist and an ER doctor I saw in a panic both assure me that, by applying silicone scar sheets to it, the swelling should reduce, and it should look normal within a few months

(and it seems to be working, as it looks much better after just a month), but much like I describe in this book, no healing process is normal. There will always be hiccups, but it's about owning these, addressing these, and dealing with these hiccups properly, instead of hiding them underneath long sleeves or masks.

I hope to continue to heal, both mentally and physically. I hope that this journey continues to be as fruitful and as fulfilling as it has been in the past year. I hope my story helps you, and I hope that someday, you can tell me your story, so I can grow from that, too.

Moving forward? I will continue to work on owning my story, wholly. When someone asks me what happened, I will work on sharing the situation without lying. I hope to continue to be honest about who I am and where I came from and where I'm going. And I hope to continue to choose to become the person I know I can grow into. Who I know I can be.

That said, while it's been fun to share my story with you—and I hope you were able to get something from it—I think I'm going to go back to writing fiction, now.

There's an idea I've been meaning to flesh out since before any of this happened—an idea scrawled onto notebook paper in 2013. It was set aside when I broke my foot while working on a production floor in 2013. It was set aside again when I got a new job, and my job got too intense from 2014–2015. And it was set aside again when my car was stolen (my notebooks and flash drives with all of my work were, conveniently, stored in my back seat) in 2016. Then of course, after Jake passed, I needed to repair myself. And so it was set aside again. While I am not writing this next idea for him, it has been in the back of my mind all this time, and this was the first idea that he said, "Yeah, I think you could probably go somewhere with that." (He was my toughest critic, but again, I appreciate him for that.)

Now that I think I'm in a good spot again (knock on wood), I think it's finally time to return to that idea—*Death's Intern Derrick*.

COVID thoughts, which I believe are still relevant

This morning, I woke up feeling helpless. Not for any reason in particular. My best guess is that it stemmed from a dream I can't fully remember. Something about an old cottage surrounded by quicksand. I was standing on the edge of its dilapidated porch, full moon, wolves howling in the distance. Beneath me, the sand was dragging the house's foundation with it, slow pull. I yelled at the morphing landscape, holding an overflowing bag of sunflower seeds that, for whatever reason, was important to me at the time. I clutched onto the bag, which caused it to burst from the bottom and the seeds to cascade onto the ground and into the quicksand. I kept yelling, trying to will it to stop, but no matter how much I yelled, the foundation kept shifting and the sunflower seeds kept falling. I couldn't stop it.

I was going to record this in my dream journal, as I've been trying to do lately, but when I looked out my bedroom window, I realized I had slept through my alarm. Not by looking at the clock, but by the angle of the sun. I wasn't late, but by the looks of it, I probably had about five minutes to get down there before I was, if that. Coffee would have to wait. Throughout the day, the dream lingered in the back of my brain as I went through the motions. I was unable to get my mind away from that scene, but I was also unable to make anything out of it. A creative stalemate.

I've always said that by 30 I want three books under my belt, which is ten months away. I thought this would be a breeze during this forced break from normal life, but it's been difficult. Hypothetically, it seems like the perfect time. But actually? It doesn't feel right. I know what I want to write, but it's difficult to concentrate on one thing when the world is shifting. It's difficult to call myself a writer while I'm actually spending most of my time watching an endless loop of It's Always Sunny in Philadelphia or The Fresh Prince of Belair, but it's even more difficult to acknowledge that this might be exactly what I need. A break.

I have to pause to say this time hasn't been terrible for me, and I feel fortunate for that. I bought a 1960s Cape Cod, well-loved and maintained by its previous owner, Kevin, who had a knack for DIY and gardening. Jason, the photographer some of you may have met on the road, is living here, too. While (as I like to say) he's jazz and I'm blues, he's my best friend, and I can't picture being stuck with anyone else through this, despite our differences. I started a new job, which has been challenging me to use a different part of my brain than I'm used to. Less creative, more logic. I've also picked up a few steady freelance jobs, which use more creativity and less logic. A balance.

I'm still working on SteVAN (the 1979 Chevy G-20 Gerring conversion van that some of you may be familiar with). Progress has been slow, but I'm learning a lot as I work towards getting him up and running again. There have been some roadblocks, but those roadblocks have forced me to actually learn the beast I will be touring in, once it's safe to do so again.

All of that said, I have to acknowledge that I am very fortunate to be where I am, especially now. It's been a productive year, and I cannot discredit the fortune of luck I've had, as I realize many haven't been this lucky.

It's difficult to feel grateful right now. 2020 has been rough, as if a tornado came through and exposed all of our structural problems. These problems, they were all there before, but now they're all front and center, sweating under the spotlight of a packed stadium. It's a helpless feeling from the audience knowing there is no concrete thing any of us can do to make things better.

These problems are not going away, and there is nothing I can do to fix them. Instead, I have to give the wheel to others who can, and I have to watch, wait, and listen to see where I can help, if I can.

This wasn't an easy revelation for me. Many of you know that I struggle with control issues. When there is a problem, I have to fix it. If I can't fix it, I hyper-focus on it until it is fixed. For example, the morning of my birthday, I yelled at Jason unsolicited, "What is the point of celebrating? There are people dying everywhere and there's nothing any of us can do to stop it. What the fuck am I celebrating? Global failure?"

This is obviously not a rational reaction, but it's difficult to be rational right now. I'm glad I had a moment of clarity that knocked me out of this negative spiraling thought-train, albeit after a two hour cry-fest curled up under my desk.

Part of this period is learning how to adjust to challenges and admit that sometimes there are situations we cannot control. This isn't something that any of us asked for, certainly not. The most important thing we can do right now is to assess the situation in front of us and proceed in a way that's best for all of us, knowing what we know now.

It is difficult to watch our friends, our family, and our neighbors suffer especially now, when everything is changing. It can be overwhelming to log into social media and see something new happen, something catastrophic, and not want to burn down every establishment that even partially contributed to whatever atrocity is trending each day. Add PTSD to the mix, and it can derail you for a day or two when you see something that triggers you. With social media, we are part of a global community, and as part of that global community, it's difficult to feel helpless when very real problems are addressed and there's little we can do about it but watch it play out.

There is a difference between reaction and action. Reaction can be reckless when we act before we know how to best proceed. Action is productive when we've digested the situation, we've listened to those who are directly affected by it, and have assessed how to move forward with intent.

For me, I don't have experience in many of the problems sitting center stage. It's been difficult for me to grasp that I cannot solve these problems if I have not experienced them first hand. In some instances, I will never know the full roots of the pain. I can only react to the surface I can see. This is not productive. This is not action because I do not have roots in these very real systemic problems. I can only react to how I feel, surface level.

I've learned to rely on those who do have these roots, and to follow their lead. I trust my friends who do have this experience, and I realize they are the only ones who will know which actions will be the most beneficial. And I've learned I cannot judge the actions of someone who understands these issues much deeper than I ever will. It is not their job to explain to me why their actions are sound. It's up to me to try to better understand their perspective and these roots, even if only a little better. That is the only way to turn reaction to action, or at least to develop some sort of productive, two-way conversation. The pain they feel is real, and the only way to better understand that pain is to listen.

While I'm sure it's clear I'm talking about everything that's happened since George Floyd was killed, this also applies to the economic crisis, the health crisis, and everything in between. I hurt for my friends who were supposed to be on the road now. I hurt for my friends who have lost their jobs due to the pandemic. I hurt for my friends who have lost loved ones from COVID-19, or have contracted COVID-19 themselves. These pains are also incredibly real. This year has been a trial for all of us, whether we've been directly impacted or not, and there is not one thing any of us can do that will make it all go away. The best thing we can do is to be there for each other and to help where we can.

I've had difficulty putting my feelings into words because I wasn't entirely sure how I felt for a majority of this time. I've been trying to summarize it or make some sense of it for the past eight months, but it's been tough. I didn't want to write something just to do it. I wanted to be sure I had intent behind my words, and I wanted to be sure I had something worthwhile to say. If this short essay accomplishes that, I guess you're all of the judge on that now. I hope it has.

This delayed drafting was not intentional, however. I have had things to say. I've written approximately seventeen different essays over the past eight months. I've come close to publishing a few, but at the last minute, they didn't ring right. So many things have happened in such a short amount of time. Whenever I start to process what I feel in a particular situation, something else would happen and cast a new light on this feeling. My perspective would shift, and my essay would then feel irrelevant under that new light.

These essays have been similar to the bag of sunflower seeds in my dream. I'd grasp onto them, grasp too tight as things changed, then the bag would burst. And in retrospect, much like the sunflower seeds in my dream, they became irrelevant as soon as they sunk beneath new foundation, whether I liked it or not. We can't get them back, no matter how hard we try. We can't keep yelling at the shifting foundation. We have to address the fact that the foundation is shifting and proceed from there in a way that's best for all of us, knowing that information we know now. We can't keep yelling at what we don't have anymore, or ignore the situation in front of us only to sink with it.

What we can do is address that our own individual problems are still valid. It isn't selfish to take care of yourself during this time. Looking globally, the only way you can help others is if you help yourself first. There's no way you can help anyone up if we're scratching from the bottom of the well yourself. Looking personally, there isn't anything one person can do individually to solve any of these problems. It would be arrogant to think any of us can solve this on our own. It would also be incredibly stressful, and I wouldn't wish the burden of all of this on any one person.

Past that, the most important thing to do right now is to listen, and to act with intent rather than react with impulse. The only place we can do that from is a solid platform. This quicksand that is 2020 may level the house we're standing in now, but hopefully a field of sunflowers will spring up in its place from the seeds we've dropped. Who knows.

Even if this doesn't happen, we should probably focus on rebuilding on stronger ground, rather than continuing to build where we just sunk. The only way we can appreciate that is to be present, to care for ourselves, and to help our friends and neighbors out when they need it, as best we can.

It's been a rough one, but we will make it through this. In the meantime, take care of yourself as best you can, listen to yourself, listen to others, and if you need it, ask for help. It is not weak to ask for help in the middle of an economic crisis, a health crisis, and a systemic crisis. This is not selfish to want stability for yourself, even if the rest of the world seems unstable. It is the only way we can build stronger, together.